Expository Sermons on the Book of
DANIEL

THE BOOKS OF DR. CRISWELL . . .

Expository Sermons on Revelation
The Holy Spirit in Today's World
The Bible for Today's World
Did Man Just Happen?
In Defense of the Faith
Our Home in Heaven
Expository Notes on the Gospel of Matthew

Expository Sermons on the Book of DANIEL

by W. A. Criswell

ZONDERVAN PUBLISHING HOUSE
Grand Rapids, Michigan

Expository Sermons on the Book of Daniel, Volume I

Library of Congress Catalog Card Number 68-27468

Printed in the United States of America

DEDICATION

TO THE MEMORY OF MRS. VELMA L. BARNETT

whose loving devotion to her husband, Mr. A. S. Barnett, was an example for every married couple, and whose quiet faithfulness to the work of our Lord was an inspiration and a blessing to us all.

FOREWORD

Having preached through the Book of the Revelation (these sermons were published by Zondervan in five volumes), I gave myself to the dedicated assignment of preaching through the Book of Daniel. As I entered into the study, I was overwhelmed by the immensity and virulence of the bitter attacks against the authenticity of this prophecy. In the liberal world the Book is universally rejected as a fraud and a forgery. This is enough in itself to make a Bible-believing and Bible-preaching pastor such as I pause long and intently before what is so seriously and arrogantly avowed by so many.

Instead of plunging into the text of the Book, therefore, I began to read the "pros" and the "cons" of the arguments concerning its composition. This perusal led to still other studies and inquiries, until finally I found myself preaching a series of introductory sermons on the author, the background, the history, the language, the critical questions and other related matters that so largely framed the Book and its inclusion in the Old Testament canon.

During those days of preaching, Mr. Pat Zondervan came to see me from Grand Rapids, Michigan, the home of the Zondervan Publishing House. When he saw what I was doing, he strongly suggested that these introductory sermons be printed in a volume separate and apart. His suggestion has been carried out. This first volume on Daniel is composed of those messages delivered for the purpose of presenting the whole, vast ferment of the theological world concerning the author and the visions in this most rejected of all the books in the Bible.

Would you be interested in what the liberals say concerning the Book of Daniel? They have written a library on the subject, but what they say is nothing but a re-hashing of what was said by the pagan philosopher, Porphyry, centuries ago in his caustic and scathing rejection of Christianity. An easily accessible presentation of the liberal point of view can be found in the world-famed *Expositor's Bible*, the commentary on "The Book of Daniel," by the Very Reverend Frederick W. Farrar, D.D., F.R.S., one time canon of Westminster and later dean of Canterbury. What he writes he writes skillfully, effectively and devastatingly. Never was so hard a steel fist covered with so soft a glove. But with all his pious words about the spiritual value of the Book, he leaves it in shambles. It is still a forgery and a fraud according to Dean Farrar.

Would you like to read a modern classic on the historicity and authenticity of the Book of Daniel? Among many others, choose the volume, *In and Around the Book of Daniel* by Charles Boutflower, a Zondervan reprint of 1963. It will thrill your heart to read of the confirming historical and archaeological discoveries recounted in this volume by Boutflower, which verify the details of the life and times depicted in Daniel. We are not alone in lining up with our Lord when He spoke of "the prophet Daniel." A thousand thousand witnesses cry out their confirmation to the truth of our Saviour as each artifact and piece of pottery and baked brick and ancient inscription adds its full measure of testimony to the truth of the prophecy. There has been no spade-full of dirt turned up by the archaeologist's shovel but that confirms the facts we read in this first of all apocalypses. God Himself gave these visions to His prophet-statesman Daniel and the centuries since in unfolding history and in inscriptional evidence attest to the inspiration of the heavenly message.

The next volume I shall publish on Daniel will be an exposition of the text itself. I am already preaching these sermons. How pertinent they are to these heavy days in which we live! You would think Daniel was writing the headlines for our daily newspapers. God's message is timeless in time, eternal in eternity. God's Word is like God Himself, the same yesterday and today and forever. Heaven and earth may pass away, but God's Word will never pass away.

Let me express my profound gratitude to Dr. Bruce Waltke, a fellow-elder in our dear church, a brilliant Ph.D. in Semitic languages from Harvard, and a Professor of Hebrew and Assyriology at the Dallas Theological Seminary, for his invaluable assistance to me as I wrestled with some of the critical problems of the Book. Without his direction, some of the conclusions reached in this series of messages could not have been historically, linguistically and archaeologically maintained. I am his debtor forever. And let me thank Mrs. Elcyee Mae Brister, a certified court reporter and a beloved member of our congregation, whom one of our deacons, Mr. Dave Wicker, Jr., sent to me to type out the sermons as I delivered them. God bless you all for your invaluable help.

And God bless you who read these pages. These are evil times for the Word of the Lord. God's Holy Book is denied, denounced, decimated, dissected, destroyed on every hand. But it endures and shall through all ages. Isaiah spoke by inspiration from heaven when he said, "The grass withereth, the flower fadeth: but the word of our God shall stand forever." Amen.

W. A. Criswell

Pastor's Study
First Baptist Church
Dallas, Texas

CONTENTS

Expository Sermons on the Book of ***DANIEL***

CHAPTER 1

WHY THE CRITICS ASSAIL THE BOOK OF DANIEL

> . . . and Daniel had understanding in all visions and dreams.
>
> Daniel 1:17

There is not a liberal theologian in the world, past or present, who accepts the authenticity of the Book of Daniel. They all deny its integrity, declaring the Book to be a blatant, patent forgery. They define its contents as pure, unadulterated fiction. This pattern of denial has continued for years and years.

We ask, Why this increasing and vicious attack against the Book? The answer is clear and plain. The Book is discredited because of the attempt on the part of modern rationalism to destroy the supernatural and the prophetic in the Bible. The ultimate aim of the destructive critic is to make of the Bible a human book like any other book. They start with Daniel for two reasons:

1. Daniel, to them, is the most vulnerable to criticism of all the books in the sacred canon.

2. Whatever else the destructive critics may achieve in their attacks, if the Book of Daniel is left intact, they have failed. No thesis against the supernatural in the Bible could survive as long as Daniel stands. The visions and the miracles in the Book of Daniel are presentations of deeds and facts that only God could know or do. If the prophetic and the supernatural in the Bible are to be removed, then Daniel must be destroyed.

I. Prophecy in the Bible

For a moment, let us look at prophecy in the Bible.

1. Prophecy is everywhere in and throughout the Word of God. It is not incidental or peripheral. It is central and dynamic. It colors everything throughout the Sacred Book. The predictive element, like a Gulf Stream, makes its way from shore to shore in the ocean of God's truth. From the beginning to the end, from time to eternity, from Genesis to Revelation, prophecy is a facet of God's Word. One gifted writer avows that two-thirds of the Scriptures are prophetic either in type, symbol or direct statement. This scholar also adds that more than one-half of the prophecies are yet to be fulfilled.

2. Prophecy is unique to the Bible. All other religious books contain no predictions as to the future. If their human authors had attempted to foretell the future, their errors, mistakes, misguesses, and unfulfillments would long ago have discredited their writings. Only the Bible has prophecy. Only God knows the future. In no small measure the Holy Scripture bases its authority, authenticity and inspiration on prophecy.

For example, Jesus said to His disciples in the dark night before Gethsemane: "And now I have told you before it come to pass, that, when it is come to pass, you might believe" (John 14:29). Though betrayed and delivered to death, the Son of man was yet to be accepted as the Son of God by the forlorn disciples because His words of prophecy would come true. The sign of His true character was to be verified by His true predictions.

We have another example of this authority of the Word proved by fulfillment of prophecy in the address of Moses in Deuteronomy 18:19-22: "And it shall come to pass, that whosoever will not harken unto my words which he (the True Prophet) shall speak in my name, I will require it of him. But the prophet, which shall presume to speak a word in my name, which I have not commanded him to speak, or that shall speak in the name of other gods, even that prophet shall die. And if thou say in thine heart, How shall we know the word which the Lord hath not spoken? When a prophet speaketh in the name of the Lord, if the thing follow not, nor come to pass, that is the thing which the Lord hath not spoken, but the prophet hath spoken it presumptuously: thou shalt not be afraid of him." According to Moses, then, the way to differentiate between a true and a false prophet is to see whether what he predicts comes to pass or not.

This trial by fire to set apart true prophets from false prophets is certainly followed in the Bible. Who is right and who is wrong, who speaks the Word of the Lord and who speaks falsely, when Micaiah is confronted by Zedekiah in the dramatic story recorded in I Kings 22:1-38? God's Word is proved to be in the mouth of Micaiah when King Ahab is slain and Zedekiah hides himself in an inner chamber for shame (I Kings 22:25). Who speaks for God and who speaks presumptuously when Jeremiah is contradicted by Hananiah in the tragic days of national loss recorded in Jeremiah 28:10-17? The nation goes into captivity and Hananiah dies within seven months according to the word of Jeremiah. The fulfillment of prediction is the sign of the true prophet. It is even as the Scriptures record of the youthful Samuel: "And Samuel grew, and the Lord was with him, and did let none of his words fall to the ground" (I Samuel 3:19).

Prophecy is history written in advance. Only God could possess such foreknowledge. Daniel thus declared the truth to King Nebuchadnezzar when he said, "the great God hath made known to the king what shall come to pass hereafter" (Daniel 2:45). God alone could reveal such a secret.

Prophecy is twofold. It is exhortative, sermonic, full of appeal to the people as God pleads for righteousness, justice, and obedience. It is also predictive, unveiling the future, as God makes known to men what shall certainly come to pass. "And the dream is certain, and the interpretation thereof sure" (Daniel 2:45). The prophets were both forth-tellers and foretellers. They possessed both insight and foresight. Their utterances were not the deductions of reason but were imparted to them by the Holy Spirit. Peter outlined this truth: "For the prophecy came not in old time by the will of man: but holy men of God spake as they were moved by the Holy Ghost" (II Peter 1:21).

3. If the predictive element in prophecy can be seen in other Books of the Bible, it is particularly and especially prominent in Daniel. If prophecy can be likened to a great river making its ever widening way through the Bible, then it can be said that the river broadens and deepens into veritable seas in two Books of the Sacred Word: Daniel and the Revelation. Both Books are viciously and violently attacked, but especially the Book of Daniel.

II. The Attack Aganist the Fulfillment of Prophecy

How could an attack be mounted against plain, simple prophecy that has been fulfilled? *Here* on this page of the Bible the prediction is made. *There* in the after years of history the prophecy has been fulfilled. How does a critic deny that? How can he destroy that?

The critic can say of the miraculous passage of Israel through the Red Sea that the people actually waded through a swampy "Reed Sea" and nothing of the miraculous attended the escape. The critic can say of the manna in the wilderness that the phenomenon was nothing but common sap oozing from a desert plant and in that instance happened to be nutritious enough to sustain life. The critic can say of the fire that fell from heaven on Elijah's Mt. Carmel offering that a chance volt of lightning happened to strike the sacrifice at that particular moment. The critic can say of the resurrection of Jesus from the dead that the disciples were victims of hallucinations and that they just "thought" they saw the living Jesus. The critic can say of Paul's conversion on the road to Damascus that he had a sunstroke, or, as many of them say, he had an epileptic fit. But of prophecy, of prediction that is fulfilled, what could the critic say to deny so patent a fact? Surely, surely this is a sign from heaven that could not be denied, even as God's Word says it cannot be denied (Deuteronomy 18: 19-22; John 14:29). What can the critic say to so plain a truth?

1. *Porphyry showed the way*

The answer to the question, How can an attack be made against fulfilled prophecy, was made by a heathen philosopher who bitterly confronted the Christian faith centuries ago. His name is Porphyry. Let us become acquainted with this amazing man.

Porphyry was born in A.D. 233 in Tyre, Syria. He studied for a while under the great church father, Origen, in Caesarea, Palestine, from which fact it is supposed that at one time he might have professed to have been a Christian. He left the school of Origen to make his way to Rome and in that capital city studied under the world famous Neo-Platonic philosopher, Plotinus, of whom he became a passionate disciple and whose teachings he popularized throughout the Empire. He was a diligent student distinguished by great learning and endowed with a gift for historical and philosophical research. In his defense of polytheism, of national religions and the worship of the popular gods, he felt, along with his fellow Neo-Platonists, that their great enemy was Christianity. He felt called upon to uproot the false teaching of Christ. In his dedication to this calling to destroy Christianity he wrote fifteen books which he entitled *Against the Christians*. The bitter volumes gained for him the reputation of being the most rabid and wicked of all the enemies of the faith.

Now Porphyry had a penchant for research. With his untiring willingness to dig back into original sources, he directed his assault against the Sacred Books of the Christians. This, therefore, is what brought his attack against Daniel. He purported to prove that the Book was not prophecy at all, that it was not written by Daniel, that it was not written during the Exile in the sixth century but was rather a forgery composed by some unknown Jew who lived about 165 B.C. during the Maccabean period and that all the events of which it prophesied had already come to pass before it was written. The whole sordid thing, Porphyry said, was a spurious lie pawned off four hundred years after it was supposed to have been composed.

The acrimonious words of Porphyry were an insult to the Christian faith. His works were publicly destroyed by Emperor Theodosius II in A.D. 448. Thereafter, his attack found no repercussion in the main stream of Christianity for hundreds and hundreds of years.

2. *The modern rationalist takes up the caustic mantle of Porphyry*

Porphyry had no effect upon the vigorous conquests of Christianity for centuries; that is, until the birth of German rationalism. But in their efforts to destroy the miraculous and the supernatural in the Bible, the German higher critics turned to Porphyry and repeated his vicious attacks against the Book of Daniel. After all, Satan has no new inventions. He uses the same old devices he has always employed from the days of the Garden of Eden when he cast doubt upon the Word of God (Genesis 3:1). Nor are there any new arguments to be presented against the Christian faith. Celsus said them all around A.D. 150. It is thus with the higher critics today. They have nothing new to report. They just rewrite as their own the conclusions of heathen philosophers who preceded them. Thus modern infidels mouth the objections of Porphyry. He said Daniel was a forgery and that is what they say. The astonishing development, however, is that the denials of Porphyry have become universally accepted among all liberal-minded theologians of our generation. His reasons are taught in the classroom and his deductions are received as truth by the whole liberal, academic world.

This principle of denial to God that He reveals the

specific future is applied to all the Bible. When the same higher critics read the name "Cyrus" in Isaiah 44:28 and Isaiah 45:1 they immediately and hastily avow that such a revelation is impossible. The prophecy must have been written *after* Cyrus lived. They conclude, therefore, that there must have been two or three or more Isaiahs, each living in different centuries and each without the gift of prophecy, but rather each writing history as though it were prophecy. There is no end to this destructive method that seeks to reduce the Holy Scriptures to a common human denominator, making of the Bible a book like any other book.

3. *Why the critics' attack is a concern to us*

Why should we concern ourselves with what the critics say? Even if their words were true, what of them? There are several deeply moving reasons for our perturbation.

(a) Jesus called Daniel, in Matthew 24:15, "a prophet." He did not say "Daniel the forger" or "Daniel the deceiver" but He said, "Daniel the prophet." If the visions of Daniel are past history clothed in the garb of prophecy and pawned off four hundreds years after they were supposed to have been written, then Daniel was no prophet. But Jesus said he was "a prophet."

(b) Daniel is the indispensable introduction to the New Testament, and especially to New Testament prediction, and most especially to the Revelation. The Book of Daniel is woven into the very warp and woof of New Testament prophecy. To understand Jesus and Paul and John, we must understand Daniel.

Sir Isaac Newton, the great scientist who discovered the law of gravity, wrote in his book, *Observations Upon the Prophecies of Daniel and the Apocalypse of St. John,* these words: "Whoever rejects the prophecies of Daniel does as much as if he undermined the Christian religion, which, so to speak, is founded on Daniel's prophecies of Christ." Bishop Westcott declared that no other book of the Old

Testament had so great a share in the development of Christianity. Paul's predictions of the anti-Christ, Bishop Westcott said, point back to the visions of Daniel. John's Revelation is largely based on Daniel. The Apostle John is the Daniel of the New Testament. The Book of Daniel and the Apocalypse of John stand or fall together.

(c) The Book of Daniel is a classic of the very highest character. Reading it again and again, we gain the distinct impression of God's presence and voice in it. The Bible would be incomplete without it. God, Himself, gave the visions and God, Himself, placed them in the canon of the Holy Scriptures.

The attack upon the Book of Daniel, therefore, is founded upon the exigencies and necessities of modern rationalism. The visions of Daniel afford an unanswerable testimony to the reality of inspiration and the reality of the supernatural. Daniel's voice must be stilled if the case of the higher critic is to stand. For every miracle in the Bible the critic finds a natural cause. Wherever a Messianic passage is found in the Old Testament (such as the fifty-third chapter of Isaiah), the critic will reject its Messianic interpretation. But if the visions of Daniel were truly, verily seen in the sixth century B.C. then skepticism becomes impossible. This accounts for the violence of the attack against the Book. The propaganda to degrade the Bible to the common level of a human book finds its best expression in the necessity to prove that Daniel was written *after* the events which it professes to predict had come to pass.

(d) There is one other reason why the attack of the modern rationalist is a concern to us. It is this: to destroy prophecy is to destroy the Bible. Christianity is a revealed religion or it is nothing at all. Job 11:7 declares that man, by searching, cannot find God. If we are to know God, God must reveal Himself. The Bible is the record of that self-disclosure of the Almighty Creator. To take that supernatural self-disclosure out of the Bible is to destroy the religion itself. The attempt to make the Christian religion but man's search for God is to lower our faith to the level of any other philosophical system of which the world already has too many.

But Christianity is alone, separate, unique, apart, exalted, holy. And this uniqueness can best be seen in the prophets. Read again the presentation of Christ as He was seen by the eye-witness Simon Peter, then stand amazed with me as Peter adds: "We have also a more sure word of prophecy; whereunto ye do well that ye take heed, as unto a light that shineth in a dark place, until the day dawn, and the day star arise in your hearts" (II Peter 1:19). Beyond the testimony of the actual eye-witness of the glories of the Son of God, is the testimony of the prophecies in Holy Scripture! What an amazing thing!

Let us read again Luke 24:13-48 and notice in Luke 24:27 and in Luke 24:44, 45 how the Lord proved His Messianic ministry out of the prophecies in the Old Testament. "And beginning at Moses and all the prophets, he expounded unto them in all the scriptures the things concerning himself." "And he said unto them, These are the words which I spake unto you, while I was yet with you, that all things must be fulfilled, which were written in the law of Moses, and in the prophets, and in the psalms, concerning me." This was Christ's way of preaching and proving that He was the true Messiah; namely, that He was the fulfillment of prophecy (compare Luke 4:16-21). This was also the way of preaching in the days of the apostles. So Acts 3:24: "Yea, and all the prophets . . . have likewise foretold of these days." So Acts 10:43: "To him give all the prophets witness, that through his name whosoever believeth in him shall receive remission of sins." So Acts 26:22, 27: "Having therefore obtained help of God, I continue unto this day, witnessing both to small and great, saying none other things than those which the prophets and Moses did say should come. . . . King Agrippa, believest thou the prophets? I know that thou believest."

If the prophecies are not true, Christianity is not true. To destroy the prophets is to destroy Christ. As it was in the days of the Apostle John when he wrote the Apocalypse, so it is God's truth to us today and ever shall be: "the testimony of Jesus is the spirit of prophecy" (Revelation 19:10). And Daniel had the spirit of prophecy and spoke of Jesus and of the centuries to come. This is the foundation of the faith.

CHAPTER II

DANIEL IS EATEN UP IN THE CRITICS' DEN

> Then the king commanded, and they brought Daniel, and cast him in the den of lions.
>
> Daniel 6:16

Following the methods and the conclusions of the pagan philosopher Porphyry, the rationalistic critics literally tear the Book of Daniel asunder. There is nothing in the volume they accept as authentic. The whole work is a forgery. It was written, they say, about 165 B.C., four hundred years after it purports to have been composed. They say it belongs to the Pseudepigrapha, a class of Jewish literature that appeared in the second century before Christ, a conglomerate of worthless trash which was published under assumed names, forgeries written in the form of prophecies such as "The Book of Enoch" and "The Testament of the Twelve Patriarchs." They say the Book of Daniel is just such a piece of fiction, a work of the imagination cleverly put together. Its great facts are fancies, they say. Its mighty miracles are feats of imagination. Its so-called prophecies are past history clothed in the garb of prophecy, a favorite practice of pseudepigraphic apocalypses.

The critics attack the Book of Daniel under four categories:

1. *Historical.* They say the Book is full of historical errors, inaccuracies, and anachronisms.

2. *Philological.* They say the Book is full of linguistic irreconcilables.

3. *Prophetical.* They say the Book is full of prophetical impossibilities.

4. *Doctrinal.* They say the Book is full of doctrinal aberrations.

Let us listen to these ravenous critics as they tear the flesh of authenticity and inspiration from the bones of the Book of Daniel.

I. The Alleged Historical Errors

The first words of the first sentence in the Book is a springboard for their formidable assault. They like not, they believe not a thing they read, neither here in the beginning avowal nor in any other of the chapters and verses that follow.

1. Daniel 1:1 starts off with the statement, "In the third year of the reign of Jehoiakim, king of Judah, came Nebuchadnezzar king of Babylon unto Jerusalem and besieged it." The critics say that first sentence openly contradicts Jeremiah 46:2. They say there was at that date no such invasion of Judah, no such siege by Nebuchadnezzar, and no such deportation of Jewish captives as described in later verses of the chapter. We do not have time here to discuss the alleged error, but one remark can surely be made in passing: Far from being a telltale sign of the spurious nature of the Book, just the opposite is true. The author plainly says that he has the prophecies of Jeremiah before him and that he had prayerfully, deeply studied them (Daniel 9:2). It is, therefore, unthinkable that a so-called Maccabean fabricator, with Jeremiah before him, would have contradicted Jeremiah in the first sentence of his so-called "romance" (this is what the critics call the Book of Daniel). He is, rather, writing independently and from personal, contemporary knowledge. As any serious study will show, both Daniel and Jeremiah are true. Jeremiah uses the Hebrew manner of reckoning; Daniel uses the Babylonian.

2. Daniel 1:1 names "Nebuchadnezzar." The critics say

the spurious author of Daniel does not even know how to spell the king's name. They say it should be spelled "Nebuchadrezzar," spelled with an "r," but the author, not knowing how to spell his name correctly, spells it as it came to be spelled four hundred years later, showing he wrote four hundred years later than he said he wrote. But Daniel spells the name the way it is spelled in Kings, Chronicles, Ezra, and even as Jeremiah spells it half of the time.

The transliteration of Babylonian cuneiform into Hebrew and Aramaic may not always be exactly alike. (Compare the spellings of the name of the Assyrian monarch, Tiglath-pileser, Tilgath-pilneser, in II Kings 15:29; I Chronicles 5:26; II Chronicles 28:20. Compare the Greek spelling of his name, Nabochodonosor.) In any event, the change from "r" to "n" which is found in the two writings of the name in the Hebrew and the Aramaic of the Scriptures is not an uncommon practice in Semitic languages, as in Ben-hadad and Bar-hadad. The alternative Hebrew rendering Nebuchad*r*ezzar may be derived from an Aramaic form of the name. His name literally is Nabu-kudurri-usur, which possibly means, "O Nabu, protect the succession rights," or, "Nabu, protect the boundary."

3. Daniel 1:1 calls Nebuchadnezzar a "king" before his father, Nabopolassar, the king of Babylon, died. But so does Jeremiah 27:6. The son, Nebuchadnezzar, was co-sovereign with his father. This explains the "three years" of Daniel 1:5, during which Daniel and his three friends were trained in the wisdom of the Chaldees, and the "second year" of Daniel 2:1, when Daniel stood before the king as a graduate of the Chaldean schools. Nebuchadnezzar reigned conjointly with his father, Nabopolassar, for at least two years. The reckoning in Daniel 2:1 is dated from the time that he reigned alone, which would be at least the fourth year from the time he began to rule with his father. The ancient Babylonian historian Berosus states that when Nabopolassar was aged and infirm he gave the Chaldean armies to the charge of his son, Nebuchadnezzar.

4. Daniel 1:3 calls the prince of the eunuchs by the name of "Ashpenaz." The critics say that is pure fiction for no such name ever appeared in the records of ancient Babylon. But a few years ago the name was found by an Assyriologist on a canonical brick retrieved from the ruins of Babylon and now preserved in the British Museum.

5. Daniel 1:6 names "Daniel." The critics avow that no such person ever existed and most especially one in such high estate as Daniel is described as achieving, because his name is not found in the monuments of the historical records of Babylon. This argument would really destroy the existence of Moses, Jesus, Paul and practically all the rest of the great characters of the Bible. Where is there a contemporary monument or inscription of any kind in Egypt that bears the name of Moses? Where is there a contemporary reference to Jesus? Outside the New Testament literature, where would one ever learn about Paul? The truth is ever evident that the world does not judge as God judges. What is great in the eyes of contemporary historians may be nothing in the balances of the Almighty. And oh, how historians have failed to see the hand of God in the lives of His saints! A thousand thousand great men have failed to achieve recognition in the annals of men who are enrolled as heroes of the faith in the Book of Life. Among those that the Babylonians passed by in their monuments was God's greatly beloved statesman, Daniel. He, along with a multitude of forgotten engineers, generals, artisans, poets, and men of genius, are never referred to as the inscriptions of the kings recount their personal glories in the records they left behind.

6. Daniel 2:2 refers to the "Chaldeans" as a class of astrologers and magicians. The critics say this is "an immense anachronism," a dead giveaway that the Book was written centuries after it says it was. They say the word "Chaldeans" in the days of Nebuchadnezzar referred to the people of the nation of Chaldea (Babylonia) and was not used to refer to a class of astrologers until long, long after

Babylon fell. But Herodotus also uses the term as Daniel does, and he lived in the same historical era with him. Daniel uses the word both ways. In Daniel 5:30 and 9:1, he applies the word to the nation of Chaldea; in Daniel 2:2, he uses the word to refer to a class of astrologers. There must have been some reason for that. Archaeology has provided the answer. We now know that the word "Chaldeans" in Daniel's day not only referred to the nation of Babylonia, but was also used to describe a priestly caste in Babylon who served the god Bel and who formed the elite of Babylonian society.

7. Daniel 5:1 introduces us to a king named Belshazzar. Here the critics have a field day. There never lived any such man, they say. He was certainly not a king and least of all of Babylon. He was in no wise kin to Nebuchadnezzar, as Daniel 5:11 would suggest; he did not die as Daniel 5:30 describes; nor was there any such historical incident as the whole chapter about Belshazzar would lead us to believe.

In the next chapter we shall write of this.

8. Daniel 5:31 and Daniel 6:1 introduce to us a ruler named "Darius the Median." The critics say again there never was any such person or ruler as Darius the Mede, and that this represents an unforgiveable confusion of history. But somebody governed the city and the nation while Cyrus attended to other conquests and arranged for the administration of his growing empire. Several astute and impressive identifications have been made as to who this Darius was. We must wait for a final answer, however, from the spade of the archaeologist. We know that he reigned synchronously with Cyrus, the former a sub-king under the latter in the one Median-Persian Empire.

9. Daniel 6:1 says that the kingdom was divided into 120 divisions. The critics say no such arrangement was ever heard of. This, also, they avow, is pure fiction. But we must remember that our knowledge of this era in history is so meager until at this present moment it would be im-

possible to write with any certainty just how the government was divided among responsible administrators. There is nothing unreasonable in what Daniel describes.

10. Daniel 9:2 refers to "the books" (the original Hebrew has the article "the"). The critics say that comprises a reference to a completed canon of Old Testament Scriptures, which canon was not in existence until the second century B.C.; therefore, the critics aver, the Book of Daniel could not have been written before the time of the fixing of the canon. If this is true, and the Book of Daniel was forged *after* the canon was fixed and complete, how in all the world did Daniel ever get included in the canon? In Daniel 9:2 the author expressly states that he had been studying the scrolls of the prophet Jeremiah and it is these scrolls to which he refers, as well as to other portions of the Old Testament.*

But enough of these so-called historical errors. We turn now to the second category of the critics' attack against Daniel.

II. Alleged Linguistic Irreconcilables

1. In the Book of Daniel are about fifteen old Persian words and the critics say this indicates a late date of com-

---

*The critical view is that the three parts of the Jewish canon, the law, the prophets, and the writings, betray three stages of canonization. They say the law was canonized around 400 B.C., the prophets around 300-200 B. C., and the writings around A. D. 100.

The argument now follows that since Daniel is a prophetic book it rightfully belongs in the second part of the canon. However, since it is not found there, it must have been written after 200 B. C.

In all this the critics argue in a circle. First they set the date of Daniel in the period of the Maccabean (around 165 B. C.). From this date they set the final closing of the canon of the prophets as some small while before that time since Daniel was not included. Every part of this reasoning is presumptuous and fictitious.

The three divisions of the canon do not represent stages of canonization but the office of the writer. One, Moses the law-giver; two, the prophets; three, the others, as David the king and David the statesman.

position. They refer to such words as "princes" in Daniel 1:3 and the king's "meat" in Daniel 1:5. But all of these words are in keeping with Daniel's life in the Babylonian and Persian court. They are rather an argument for the early dating of the Book.

2. Daniel 2:4–7:28 is written in Aramaic while the rest of the Book is written in Hebrew. We shall write of this in a later chapter. But one observation could be made in passing. The critics say the Aramaic in Daniel is late Palestinian and indicates that the Book was composed in the middle of the second century B.C. But while they were avowing this, the Dead Sea Scrolls were discovered in the caves of Qumran. Among these scrolls are some written in the Aramaic of the Maccabean second century B.C. period. It is nothing like the Aramaic of Daniel, showing that the language of Daniel is true to its sixth century B.C. composition. Even more to the point are the Elephantine Papyri, dated in the fifth century B.C. The Aramaic of these documents corresponds with the Aramaic of Daniel.

3. Daniel 3:5 contains three Greek words. The critics scoff all over their unbelieving world as they cite these evidences of the Greek period authorship of the Book. How could it have been written in the sixth century and at the same time use Greek words? To them the argument is all-decisive. However, it is anything but decisive. There was contact between the east and the west, between the Mesopotamian and Greek civilizations, between Assyria-Babylonia and Greece for centuries and centuries. Charles Boutflower, in his volume, *In and Around Daniel,* page XVII, Table III, lists by the years and the centuries the interchange of men, soldiers, artisans, builders, and a host of others between the nations. When we look at those three Greek words and discover that they are names of musical instruments, the reason for their use is most clear. Like the Italian words "piano" and "viola," the instruments carried their original names with them wherever they were transported. For the harp and the psaltery and the dulcimer to be called such

anywhere in the ancient world is no mystery at all. They were that wherever they were played, whether in Egypt, in Greece, or in Babylon.

The use of those three (and only three) Greek words naming musical instruments emphasizes in a most unusual way the early sixth century dating of the Book. If Daniel had been written in 165 B.C., the author would have not only inserted a few Greek words but would have incorporated whole Greek ideas and expressions into his document. By 165 B.C. a Greek-speaking government had been ruling Palestine for 165 years. Greek political, administrative, and cultural words would surely find their way into the language of the subject populace. To understand the truth of this inevitable penetration, we need but to read I and II Maccabees to see the extensive intrusion of Greek thought, expression, and customs into the life of the nation. But there is nothing of this in Daniel. Absolutely nothing. There is nothing Greek in the Book but the names of these three musical instruments.*

We turn now to the third category in the critics' attack against Daniel.

III. Alleged Prophetical Impossibilities

1. In Daniel 2:31-40 and in Daniel 7:1-23 a prophecy is delivered concerning four great world empires. The critics, in keeping with their "a priori" premise that there is nothing of real prophecy in the Book, make the four kingdoms, first Babylonian, second Median, third Persian, and fourth Grecian. The critics are certain that the author does not know nor does he prophesy of the Roman Empire. The critics, having arrived at the "firm" conclusion that the Book was written in 165 B.C., proceed to make everything fit in with their theory. They treat all the visions of the Book as past

---

*It might be observed in passing that one clearly Greek word, "stater," is attested in the Aramaic of the Elephantine papyri which dates, of course, over a century before the conquests of Alexander.

history. Since Rome in 165 B.C. was not a world power (although it was beginning to emerge as one), therefore, the author could not have known of its coming. The last kingdom of the four, therefore, is Greece, because Rome had not appeared on the world horizon. This interpretation is central to the destructive, critical view.

Daniel, however, plainly and expressly says just the opposite. The critics' wrenching asunder the one Median-Persian empire into two empires does great violence to Daniel, Chapter 8, where the unity of the Median-Persian kingdom is definitely affirmed. Daniel 8:3 and Daniel 8:5 describe the ram with the two horns. Daniel 8:20 says the ram with the two horns represents the Median-Persian kingdom. This corresponds exactly with the breast and two arms of silver that Daniel saw in the great image described and interpreted in Daniel 2. The Persians subsumed the Medes in 550 B.C. Years before the fall of Babylon the Medes and the Persians were already one united empire. The four kingdoms, both in prophecy and in history, are Babylonian, Median-Persian, Greek, and Roman. Daniel says thereafter there will never be another empire that encompasses the civilized world. We have had centuries and centuries to confirm the prophecy.

2. Daniel 11:21-39 portrays in great detail the conflicts between the Seleucid kings of Syria and the Ptolemaic kings of Egypt, including the career of Antiochus Epiphanes. This, of course, is unthinkable to the rationalistic mind. They say that God does not, did not, and, apparently, could not reveal such detailed future incidents. But when I read in the Old Testament the small details that are prophesied concerning the life and death of our Lord Jesus, I wonder about the critics' abuse of the detailed prophecies in Daniel. Maybe God is abler than the critics think Him to be.*

---

*The critics point out that the predicted end of king Antiochus Epiphanes in Daniel 11:40-45 differs from the stories of his death in I and II Maccabees. They argue that these verses represent real

3. The critics make much of the fact that the Book of Daniel is not in the division of the Law in the canon of the Old Testament; nor is it in the division of the Prophets of the Old Testament, but it is in the division of the Kethuvim, the Hagiographa, the Sacred Writings. We shall discuss that later. However, the point to be made here is that Daniel is in the Bible, it is a part of the canon of the Hebrew Old Testament. It is *there* for sure and for certain. In the Qumran caves the scroll of the prophet Isaiah was found. In the same caves fragments of Daniel were found. They both belong to the canon.

We turn now to the last of the four categories in which the critics propose to annihilate the authenticity of the Book of Daniel.

IV. Alleged Doctrinal Aberrations

1. Daniel 12:2, 3 says: "And many of them that sleep in the dust of the earth shall awake, some to everlasting life, and some to shame and everlasting contempt. And they that be wise shall shine as the brightness of the firmament: and they that turn many to righteousness as the stars for ever and ever." This, of course, comprises a distinct doctrine of the resurrection of the dead. To this, also, the critics violently object, saying that such a doctrine could not have been made known in the sixth century B.C. God could not, or would not, have done it. In this the critics exhibit the same kind of a perverted mind that objects so strenuously to Job 19:25, 26: "For I know that my redeemer liveth, and that he shall stand at the latter day upon the earth; and though after my skin worms destroy this body, yet in my flesh shall I see God." They say the hopes ex-

---

prediction concerning Antiochus on the part of the author or the Book, Daniel, which was never fulfilled.

The conservatives, on the other hand, answer that characteristically the prophecy shifts from the near future to the distant future; in this case, to the final Anti-Christ.

pressed in these revelations of a life beyond the grave are far beyond the level of revelation in centuries earlier than the second century B.C. Therefore, they conclude, the Book was composed not in the sixth century as it purports to be, but in the second century. But to limit God as these critics do in their criticism of these passages is to read the Almightiness of God out of the Bible. For God to write by inspiration through His prophets these words of hope in His Blessed Book is altogether in keeping with His goodness and mercy to us. There is nothing out of character; there is nothing out of date.

2. Daniel 6:22 presents an angel. Daniel 8:16; 9:21 names Gabriel. Daniel 10:13, 21; 12:1 names Michael. All of that and the whole doctrine of angels in the Book of Daniel is highly offensive to the destructive critics. To some of them it is an adoption of a heathen system of celestial beings. To others of them it is a reflection of the supersititions that were rife among the Jews of the second century B.C. world.

Looking at the presentation in the light of the whole Bible, do we find anything about the doctrine of angels in Daniel that is beyond the spirit and the revelation of the Word of God? Yes, an angel is spoken of in Daniel 6:22. But an angel spoke to Abraham in Genesis 22:11. A vision of angels appeared to Jacob in Genesis 28:12. The angelic presence was to go before Moses and the children of Israel in Exodus 32:34. An angel did "wondrously" in the announcement to Manoah in Judges 13:15-21. An angel comforted Elijah in I Kings 19:5-7. Angels ministered to the Lord Jesus after the trial in the wilderness in Matthew 4:11. An angel encouraged the Saviour in Gethsemane in Luke 22:43. An angel sat on the great stone he rolled away from the tomb of our Lord in Matthew 28:2. An angel brought the announcement of the messenger of salvation to Cornelius in Acts 10:3. An angel delivered Simon Peter from the bondage of Herod Agrippa I in Acts 12:8-11. An angel stood by the Apostle Paul in the agony of the great storm in Acts

27:23. Why would anyone object to the angels in the Book of Daniel?

The angel Gabriel is revealed for the first time in Daniel 8:16 and 9:21. He is seen again in the marvelous good news of the birth of a child to the priest Zacharias and his wife, Elizabeth, in Luke 1:13, 19. He is seen again as he is sent from God to announce to the virgin Mary that she is to be the mother of the foretold and foreordained Messiah in Luke 1:26-38. The angel Michael is revealed in Daniel 10: 13, 21 and in Daniel 12:1. He appears again in Jude 9 and in Revelation 12:7. If there are no angels in Daniel, there are no angels anywhere else. If there is no Gabriel in Daniel, there is no Gabriel anywhere else. If there is no Michael in Daniel, there is no Michael anywhere else. When we destroy Daniel we are on our way to dissolving the fabric of the whole Word of God. It is all of a piece; it is all of a kind. If the critics can eat up Daniel in the den of destruction, they can and will inevitably devour all the prophets of God, Old Testament and New Testament. It was our Lord, Himself, who observed, "For where the carcass is, there will the vultures be gathered together" (Matthew 24:28). The loss of Daniel to the ravenous critics ultimately means the loss of the Bible, itself, to their carnivorous attack. Surely God has some better thing for us than this. In the next chapter we shall see.

Chapter III

HOW THE CRITICS FARE IN THE FIERY FURNACE

> Then these men were bound in their coats, their hosen, and their hats, and their other garments, and were cast into the midst of the burning fiery furnace.
>
> Daniel 3:21

In the previous chapter, Chapter II, we outlined some of the devastating destruction by which the rationalist critics make havoc of the Book of Daniel. Let us turn this around and see how the critics fare when they are thrown into the white heat and light of historical facts and spiritual truth. We have not opportunity in this brief space to write of all their attacks and how they emerge as they are forced through the fiery furnace of reality, but we shall discuss the most salient features of their objections as typical of them all. We shall look at the history mentioned in the Book and then we shall follow the Book in history.

I. History in the Book of Daniel

Of all the alleged historical errors in Daniel, none has been so surely labeled as gross ignorance as the references to King Belshazzar. The idea of Belshazzar has been ridiculed the most sarcastically. This figure is pure unadulterated fiction, the critics say, and they are most positive in this avowal. The historical case against Belshazzar is watertight. He is a figment of pure imagination. There was no such person, no such being, he died no such death, and there was no such history concerning him as Daniel would have us believe. Armed with all these declarations, the critics would seem to have mounted an invincible attack, bolstered by a most formidable array of troops. Good. Let us put them and their declarations in the burning white light of historical truth and see how they fare.

1. The apparent and apparently conclusive facts of the chronology of the kings of the Neo-Babylonian Empire are simply stated. They follow one another like this:

(a) After a reign of forty years, Nebuchadnezzar died in 562 B.C.

(b) Evil-Merodach, his son, succeeded to the throne and reigned about two years. He was then assassinated by his brother-in-law, Neriglissar, who ascended the throne. (Evil-Merodach is named in II Kings 25:27; Neriglissar in Jeremiah 39:3, 13 under the name of Nergal-sharezer). This brings us down to 560 B.C.

(c) Neriglissar reigned four years and died, leaving the kingdom to an infant son, Labashi-Marduk. This brings us down to 556 B.C.

(d) The infant king Labashi-Marduk was deposed after nine months by a priestly revolution and Nabonidus was made king.

(e) Nabonidus, made king in 556 B.C., reigned for seventeen years, from 556 B.C. to 539 B.C., when he was taken captive by Cyrus as the Persians conquered the Empire.

In this chronology there is absolutely no room for a king Belshazzar. It is as simple as that. The critics made their point well. They vigorously avowed that all known ancient secular sources indicate Nabonidus was the last king of Babylon. But Daniel says that Belshazzar was the last king. The critics reminded us that all known ancient historians, like Berossus and Alexander Polyhistor, say that Nabonidus was the last king of Babylon. But Daniel says that Belshazzar was the last king. The critics further declared that all known secular sources record that the last king of Babylon (Nabonidus) was not killed but, rather, was given a pension by his conquerors. But Daniel says that the last king (Belshazzar) was killed when the Persians stormed into Babylon. Belshazzar, therefore, became a classic illustration of the stupid, historical errors to be found in the fiction Book called Daniel.

2. Then the archaeologists began to dig into the ruins of the Mesopotamian Valley. Oh, what the spade has done to Daniel! Great numbers of clay tablets and other ancient inscriptions were excavated among the ruins of the city along the Euphrates River and sent to the British Museum. There learned Assyriologists began to study them. Their published announcements and discoveries were amazing.

(a) A clay tablet was found which contained the name of Belshazzar, showing that such a man actually existed.

(b) A clay tablet was found which bore the names of both Nabonidus and Belshazzar, showing that there was some connection between the two.

(c) A clay tablet was found which referred to Belshazzar as the king's son.

(d) A clay tablet was found which contained an oath taken by two businessmen sealing a contract between them. The oath was taken in the name of Nabonidus and Belshazzar. Now, in ancient Babylon, oaths were taken in the name of the reigning king. This tablet showed that Belshazzar was actually co-ruler with his father.

(e) Added to all this, recent years have brought a flood of discoveries. Belshazzar, in Babylonian cuneiform BEL-SHARRA-UTSUR, "Bel protect the king," now stands before us as a very real person, one of the leading personalities of his age. He was born in 575 B.C., the eldest son of Nabonidus. When he was fourteen years old, Nebuchadnezzar died. When he was twenty years old, his father, Nabonidus, ascended to the throne. When he was twenty years old we know he had a house of his own in Babylon. When he was twenty-four years old, mention is made of his secretary. When he was twenty-six years old, his grandfather died at the advanced age of one hundred and four years. When he was twenty-seven years old, mention is made of his steward and of his secretaries (plural). At that age of twenty-seven, we also find him in southern Babylonia as commander-in-chief of the army. At thirty years of age, we find him sending by water sheep and oxen for sacrifice to the Temple of Shamash at Sippar (up the Euphrates River). On another occasion, he sends a wedge of gold weighing one mana. In the same way, we find one of his sisters sending a silver cup weighing twenty-seven shekels. Another sister was dedicated as a votaress to the moon-god Sin in the Temple at Ur (down the Euphrates River) where he built a house for her close to the women's quarters. With increasing excavations and discoveries, more and more will be known about the personal life of Belshazzar.

3. Why was Belshazzar left king in Babylon? The reason lay in the character and personality of Nabonidus. He was a man of great cultural and religious intuition. An archaeologist and a builder and restorer of temples, he sought for inscriptions concerning the exploits of ancient kings. He searched the foundations and cornerstones of public buildings, looking for documents that revealed the past. His interest in religion was intense. His mother seems to have been a priestess in the Temple of the moon-god Sin, and we have already seen, his own daughter was dedicated to that god. This inclination on the part of Nabonidus definitely drew him away from the affairs of state.

But this is not all. Not only was Nabonidus by nature a scholar and an antiquarian, but we now know that he spent most of the years of his reign, not in Babylon, but in Tema, in northern Arabia. The summation of these providences meant one thing surely and certainly; namely, somebody had to be left in Babylon to rule the kingdom while Nabonidus was away. Who would be the sovereign more naturally chosen than his own and eldest son? This is exactly what happened, as we now know from the discovery of an inscription stating that before Nebonidus left for Tema, he entrusted the kingship to Belshazzar. Belshazzar was king in Babylon in much the same way as Nebuchadnezzar was king with his father, Nebopolassar.

These historical facts presented by the late Raymond P. Dougherty, Professor of Assyriology at Yale University, explain the strange allusion in Daniel 5:16, 29. Belshazzar, in rewarding Daniel, proposes to make him "third" ruler in the kingdom. Why not the "second"? For the very apparent reason that the first ruler was Nabonidus; the second ruler was Belshazzar; and the only way the high honor could be bestowed was to make Daniel the "third" in succession. It is amazing how Biblical truth fits together when we know all the facts.

4. The death of Belshazzar has been amply corroborated. The spade of the archaeologist has uncovered the Annalistic Tablet of Cyrus. On this cylinder the Persian king describes the fall of Babylon. The armies of Cyrus had captured Nabonidus some four months before Babylon fell. In the eyes of the people this really made Belshazzar all the more the king of the city. The Tablet of Cyrus says that Babylon was easily taken. This agrees with Daniel 5:30, 31. The Tablet also says that when Babylon fell "the king's son died." Having in his possession, as a captive, Nabonidus, it is easily seen how Cyrus so described Belshazzar. Cyrus says that the night Babylon fell "the king's son died." Daniel says that "that night Belshazzar was slain."

The astonishing results and revelations of these contemporarily written tablets and inscriptions are significant beyond our power to emphasize them. Think of it! The name of Belshazzar fell out of history completely, absolutely. Herodotus visited Babylon in about 460 B.C. and wrote of its glories, mentioning its kings and queens. But he never once named Belshazzar. He never heard of him. Nor did any other historian. How could it have been, therefore, that an unknown Jew knew all about the last forgotten king, Belshazzar, four hundred years later, if Daniel was written, as the critics say, in 165 B.C.? The answer to all this is plain. The critics are wrong. They cannot hold up their heads in the white light of the historical past. Daniel knew Belshazzar because he and the king were contemporaries. Daniel lived and wrote during those epochal days. Dr. Joseph P. Free, in his *Archaeology and Bible Study,* page 235, writes: "There is no first-rate liberal today, as far as the writer knows, who urges the old objection concerning Belshazzar. The detailed facts are that Nabonidus, in one sense the last king of Babylon, was not killed by the invading Persians, but was given a pension by his conquerors. On the other hand, Belshazzar, elevated to the position of ruler of Babylon by his father, was killed when the City of Babylon was taken, as indicated in Daniel 5:30. The matter concerning Belshazzar, far from being an error in the Scriptures, is one of the many striking confirmations of the Word of God which have been demonstrated by archaeology."

If the critics are wrong about Belshazzar, how do we know but that they are not wrong about their other watertight historical demonstrations of so-called errors and inaccuracies in the Book? Time will yet reveal many, many other references which now we do not understand. Remember, not one percent of the tablets and inscriptions that lie buried in the ruins of Babylon have been unearthed. There is much to learn. And every turn of the archaeologist's spade helps to confirm the Word of God.

II. The Book of Daniel in History

As we have reviewed a part of ancient history presented in the Book of Daniel and found it to be amazingly accurate, let us now follow the history of the Book through the succeeding centuries. Here again the critics have made their blistering attacks, but they fare no better in the witness of time than they do in the witness of archaeology. Daniel says that he lived and wrote his book in the days of the Neo-Babylonian Empire, which would be the sixth century before Christ. The scoffing liberal says that he lived (whoever "he" was) and wrote his book in the days of the Maccabees about 165 B.C., four hundred years later. Do the historical references to the Book corroborate the attack of the critics? Let us see.

1. The Book of Daniel is included in the canon of the Old Testament inspired Scriptures. It is in the Bible. No amount of casuistry or sophistry can deny that it is there. We may talk about the Torah (the Law) and about the Neviim (the Prophets) and the Kethuvim (the Writings), but after the discussions are over concerning where the Book of Daniel was placed in ancient days (as in the reference made by Josephus) or in modern days, the undeniable fact remains that the Book of Daniel is in the Bible. How did it get there?

A hundred noble works were denied inclusion in the Hebrew canon of inspired Scriptures. I Maccabees, for example, is a production of the highest excellence. It possesses an authority and a value that no other part of the Apocrypha possesses. Even Martin Luther declared it not unworthy to be reckoned among the Sacred Scriptures. But it was refused. It was not ancient enough to be included. The splendid book called Ecclesiasticus, although representing the dominant thought of the Jews at the time of its composition (around 200 B.C.), was rejected. It was not ancient enough. Even canonical books such as Proverbs, Ecclesiastes, and even Ezekiel, were challenged. But "the right of the Book of Daniel to canonicity was never called in question in the Ancient Synagogues." So avows Edersheim in his *Life and Times of Jesus the Messiah,* Vol. 11, Appendix V. From the time that there was a canon of Old Testament Scriptures Daniel has ever been in it.

The canon of the Old Testament was rigidly set. No books were included which were not believed to have been in existence in the days of Nehemiah-Malachi. The test (the rule, the measure, the canon; the word means the same through the centuries, and is the exact word in spelling and in pronunciation, whether in Hebrew, Greek, or English) of a book was whether or not it was inspired.

The Ancient Synagogue believed that inspiration ceased with the prophets and they further believed that no prophet had arisen since Malachi.

The rationalistic critics would have us believe that around 165 B.C., or at the death of the oppressive Syrian ruler, Antiochus Epiphanes, some unknown Jewish writer incorporated a history of his reign in a spurious prophecy supposed to have been delivered some four hundred years before and that the work was thereupon accepted as inspired Scripture and placed in the Hebrew canon of Old Testament Books, along with the Psalms of David and the other Holy Writings. With what stupidity and credulity those men of ancient Jewry were guilty! This in the face of the known fact that the great Synagogue of the second century before Christ was comprised of men famed for their piety and learning. They entertained extremely strict views of inspiration and were literally consumed with an intense reverence for the Holy Writings. Yet the critics would have us believe that these devout scholars smuggled into the canon a book which was a forgery, a literary fraud, a fictitious novel of contemporary date! Imagine a meeting of theologians to discuss the proposal to add Bruce Barton's *The Man Nobody Knows* to the four gospels of the New Testament! No less grotesquely ridiculous is the suggestion that the Great Synagogue in the second century B.C. would have entertained the idea of adding a forged romance of their own age to the canon of the Old Testament.

2. As we follow the history of the Book of Daniel, we inevitably meet the Septuagint Greek Translation of the Old Testament Scriptures. This is the most famous and the most influential translation since the beginning of human speech. It was the Bible of the Apostles (Acts 8:35; 18:24, 28 and the Old Testament text of the Book of Hebrews). This translation from Hebrew into Greek was made under the Ptolemies in Egypt about 300 B.C. Some scholars say it was completed by 275 B.C. Is the Book of Daniel in the Greek Septuagint? It is. Yet the critics would have us believe that the Book of Daniel was not written until over

one hundred years after the Septuagint came into existence!

3. Tracing the Book of Daniel through the centuries, we find references to it in I Maccabees. This noble work was composed soon after the time they say Daniel was forged, yet the book quotes Daniel as one would Holy Scripture. I Maccabees 1:54 refers to Daniel 9:27; 11:31; 12:11 in its reference to "the abomination of desolation," as Jesus does in Matthew 24:15. Again, I Maccabees 2:49-70 comprises one of the most striking, solemn passages in the book, the record of the dying words of the venerable priest Mattathias to his sons, especially to Judas Maccabaeus. In this dying charge the noble patriot turns to the example of Daniel and his three faithful friends, to encourage his sons to be true to the God of their fathers. This is a tremendous witness to the early and authentic date of Daniel.

4. Josephus throughout his histories makes much of the Book of Daniel. The Jewish historian was a contemporary of Paul and John. In about A.D. 80 Josephus wrote the story of his people from Abraham down to the destruction of Jerusalem in A.D. 70. One of the most moving and beautiful narratives in all literature is his story of the sparing of the holy city by Alexander the Great during the latter's conquest of the Persian Empire. It is recounted in his *Antiquities of the Jews,* Book XI, Chapter 8, paragraphs 4, and 5. The conquering Alexander, during his siege of Tyre, had made appeal to the Jews for provisions for his army. Jaddua, the high priest, refused, saying that he had sworn to be faithful to Darius, the Persian king. This made Alexander furious. After his destruction of Tyre and after his destruction of Gaza, Alexander turned the wrath of his invincible army against Jerusalem. Jaddua, the high priest, was terrified, but God told him in a dream how to save the city. Carrying out the instructions of the Lord, Jaddua dressed his priests in white. He, himself, put on his glorious garments with scarlet robe, breastplate and golden mitre. Followed by a procession of priests and people in white, he went out to meet Alexander, singing the songs of Zion.

The Macedonian was overwhelmed, and especially so when Jaddua showed him Daniel 8:1-8 and Daniel 8:15-22, passages that foretold his coming and his victories. The narrative continues, saying that Alexander worshiped God and offered sacrifices in the Temple. All that happened around 330 B.C., yet the critics say Daniel was not written until 165 B.C. and that Josephus is a liar!

Whatever we may believe about Josephus being the world's greatest liar (yet he is one of the most significant historians of all time), the fact remains: namely, that while Alexander destroyed every city in Syria friendly to Darius, the Persian, yet he not only spared Jerusalem but greatly favored it. Why? There must be a reason. It is Josephus who tells us why and that "why" included the prophecies of Daniel.

5. We must hasten our summary of the Book of Daniel in history and come to our modern day. Within recent years, in the caves of Qumran, at the north end of the Dead Sea, many scrolls of ancient Biblical times and literature have been discovered. Among the scrolls are the prophecies of Isaiah and fragments of the Book of Daniel. The scrolls date back practically to the time the critics say that Daniel was forged. The scrolls of Daniel are the same as ours today, written partly in Hebrew and partly in Aramaic, and the Aramaic is not at all the Aramaic of the other documents of the Maccabean period, but the eastern Aramaic of the sixth century B.C. Where the Bible is, where Isaiah is, there Daniel is. And the Hebrew language of Daniel in the Qumran Scrolls is the good, classical, Biblical Hebrew of the Old Testament, not the Hebrew of the Maccabean period.

We are reminded of the days and the years when the critics scoffed at the thought that the Apostle John wrote the Gospel that bears his name. It was utterly impossible, they avowed, because the theological ideas concerning Christ evidenced in the Book would take at least two hundred years to develop; therefore, the gospel of John could not have been written in the first Christian century. While the critics were mouthing these things, a papyrus, dated about A.D. 90 or 95, was unearthed in Egypt, quoting the gospel of John! Moreover, these same motifs once alleged to point to a late date are now found in the Qumran Scrolls.

6. Daniel lays before us the course and the sweep of human history. We have had thousands of years to verify whether his prophecy is of God. Does history confirm or deny the visions of the Jewish captive? Whatever we may think of Daniel, himself, that he was a pious forger or not, this everlasting truth obtains: history follows the mold set for it by Daniel. As in the vision of the great image of a man, recorded in Daniel 2:31-45, the four mighty empires expressed by the head of gold, the breast and arms of silver, the thighs of brass, and the legs of iron, are followed by the iron and clay of the ten toes, the breaking up of the kingdoms of the world into separate nationalities. Following the empire of the iron legs. Daniel says there will never be another world kingdom until Messiah sets up the kingdom of God in the earth. Is this true? Does history corroborate the prophecy? Emphatically so! The last world kingdom was the divided eastern and western Roman Empire; there has never been another. Neither the United States nor Russia nor China nor any other nation will ever be able to conquer the earth.

In the extension of human history Daniel avows that "unto the end wars and desolations are determined" (Daniel 9:26 RV). Is that true? We have had centuries to judge the prophecy. What do you think?

In February of 1914, in Los Angeles, California, a group of devout Bible scholars convened in a prophetic conference. They called attention to the Scriptures which described the nations as rising in war against each other, and those holocausts followed by famine and pestilence. "For nation shall rise against nation, and kingdom against kingdom: and there shall be famines, and pestilences, and earthquakes in divers places" (Matthew 24:7). "And ye shall hear of wars and rumors of wars" (Matthew 24:6). The editor of the *Christian Advocate*, hearing of the pronouncement, ridiculed the men and their message, saying that instead of a "Prophetic Conference" it ought to be called a "Pathetic Conference." This was in February of 1914, when the liberal world was about to bring in the millennium, according to their superior theology. In less than six months the archduke of Austria was assassinated in Serbia and the whole world was engulfed in flames of fury and drowned in floods of blood. It was then that the President of the United States called for American troops to cross the seas to fight "a war to end all wars" and "to make the world safe for democracy." How hollow the words seem now after Hitler and Tojo and Stalin. How empty the words seem now in our present divided world.

It is difficult to deny the truth of God expressed in Daniel. It is sort of like a gnat climbing up the slopes of Mt. Everest, with the confident boast that he will pulverize the Himalayan Peak with the stomping of his left hind foot! It is hard to do. And the critics have a hard time. They confront their own lying prophecies and their own words mock them with inexorable confusion. They live in a fog and a mist, groping for the wall like a man born blind. Oh, how we all need the light of the knowledge of God that shines in the face of His prophets!

Chapter IV

WILL THE REAL DANIEL STAND UP?

> . . . a vision appeared unto me, even unto me Daniel, after that which appeared unto me at the first.
>
> Daniel 8:1

Who is this "me, Daniel"? His Book is in the Bible, no denying that. His prophecy is one of the greatest, most meaningful of all time. No denying that, either. But who is this "Daniel" who wrote it? The author, himself, says that he was a Jewish captive taken to Babylon by king Nebuchadnezzar, and that he lived in the court of the ruling Empire throughout the length of the Jewish captivity and down into the reign of Cyrus the Persian. Modern liberal scholarship, however, denies every syllable of this. The rationalistic critics say that "Daniel" was an unknown Jew who wrote the forgery in 165 B.C. in the days of the Maccabees, garbing it in prophecy as though it were written four hundred years earlier. This blasphemous attack has carried with it the whole liberal world. It is a part of the modern denial of the inspiration of the Holy Scriptures. We are aghast before it. Not because of the attack itself, for Porphyry voiced that brilliantly and learnedly in A.D. 275. But Porphyry was a pagan philosopher and a bitter enemy of the Christian faith.

Today, who are these leading the destructive assault against Daniel? Who are they? The infidels? No. The atheists? No. The communists? No. The attack on the Bible today is made by the preacher and the professor in the liberal pulpit and the liberal seminary. The man who is supposed to deliver the Word of God denies that there is any such thing. The man who preaches Daniel denies that Daniel ever existed, except as a fraudulent forger. To the critics "Daniel," whoever he was, lived in another day and in another time than he purports to have lived in his Book. Will the real Daniel stand up!

I. Daniel as the Supposed Fictitious Prophet of the Maccabean Period

Whoever wrote the Book of Daniel was a tremendous genius, unexcelled and unsurpassed except by the heavenly endowment of the Lord Jesus Christ. When did such a prophet live? What effect did he have as he delivered his message to his people? Who knew him and who received him?

1. The liberal world of higher criticism unanimously says that this "Daniel" lived in the days of the Maccabees. We have a marvelous account of that period in Jewish history in one of the most trustworthy documents ever to be placed in the hands of man. I Maccabees is that history. The recurring lament of I Maccabees is that "there is no prophet in the land." The dirge is voiced again and again.

(a) In the fourth chapter of I Maccabees is recorded the new dedication of the Temple after it had been defiled by the Syrian king, Antiochus Epiphanes, who had turned it into a Greek shrine to the heathen god Jupiter. Completely to violate the Jewish reverence for the holy place, Antiochus offered a sow on the great altar and poured the juice over every section of the sanctuary. When Judas Maccabeus defeated the armies of Antiochus and won back the holy places, his first act was to cleanse the earthly sanctuary in Jerusalem. The dramatic story in I Maccabees 4:44-46 is as follows: "And they took counsel concerning the altar of burnt offerings which had been profaned, what they should do with it: and there came into their mind a good counsel, that they should pull it down, lest it ever be a reproach to them: and they pulled down the altar and laid up the stones in the mountains of the house in a convenient place, until there should come a prophet to give answer concerning them." There is no prophet in the land, no Daniel to deliver the message of the Lord.

(b) In the ninth chapter of I Maccabees is recorded the death of the mighty warrior and hero, Judas Maccabeus. As the nation mourned over the loss of their great leader and as the fruits of his victories seemed about to be lost in the ravages of the apostates, I Maccabees 9:27 says, "And there was great tribulation in Israel, such as was not since the time that no prophet appeared unto them." Again, there is no prophet in the land, no Daniel to strengthen and comfort his people with a message from the Lord.

(c) In the fourteenth chapter of I Maccabees is recorded the story of the selection of Simon, the second son of Mattathias, to carry forward the struggle of the Jewish nation for survival. The record reads in I Maccabees 14:41, ". . . the Jews and the priests were well pleased that Simon should be their leader and high priest forever, until there should arise a faithful prophet." Again, there is no prophet in the land, no Daniel to direct the people.

2. As there was no prophet during the Maccabean era, so there was no prophet throughout the course of the inter-Biblical period.

From the days of Nehemiah-Malachi to the showing of John the Baptist to Israel there arose no spokesman for God in the land. Yet we have this incomparable Book of Daniel before us, and it is a part of the Bible. Where is the prophet who could have written it during that expanse of time? We look in vain throughout the corridors of the centuries of the inter-Biblical period for such a man. To search among the remains and traditions of Hebrew history is fruitless in revealing such a writer, such a seer, such a prophet. He did not exist during those days.

3. No less fortuitous is the persuasion of the critics

that an unknown forgerer could have smuggled his book into the Hebrew Old Testament canon. There was no such work added to the canon which was written after the days of Nehemiah-Malachi. The Ancient Synagogue looked upon Ezra in their traditions as the one who fixed and closed the canon. That an unknown forger named "Daniel" should have been able to write a spurious romance and get it accepted among the inspired books of the Holy Scriptures is beyond imagination. Such a thing never happened and the unknown Jew who assumed the name "Daniel" never existed. The only Daniel we have is the Daniel of the Biblical Book called by his name, and that Daniel lived during the Babylonian captivity, four hundred years before the days of the Maccabees.

II. Daniel As the Faceless Author of a Pseudepigraphon

The Pseudepigrapha refers to a collection of spurious, counterfeit Jewish writings that appeared from about 250 B.C. to about A.D. 200. The books claim to have been written by some ancient Biblical worthy whose name had been revered through the centuries. They are mostly apocalyptic in character; that is, the message is delivered in visions and in symbols, as in the Book of Daniel in the Old Testament and as in the Book of Revelation in the New Testament. Many times these false writings known as "The Pseudepigrapha" are referred to as "pseudepigraphic apocalypses." Their actual authors are completely unknown. The men who wrote them seem to have been closely associated with each other. They generally resemble each other and are mutually dependent upon each other. Seemingly they all belonged to one sect of the Jews. They were not Sadducees, they were not Pharisees. They probably were Essenes. Their books constituted the secret, esoteric wisdom of their fraternity.

Without exception, the actual author wrote under the name of some ancient Biblical character. This can be seen in the titles of the books themselves. Look at this list of writings from the Pseudepigrapha:

The Testament of Adam
The Testament of Abraham
The Testament of Job
The Testaments of the Twelve Patriarchs
The Books of Enoch
The Assumption of Moses
The Ascension of Isaiah
The Apocalypse of Baruch
The Psalter of Solomon
The Odes of Solomon
The Fourth Book of Ezra

These writings are plainly spurious and are excluded from the canon of the Old Testament. They are not even included in the Apocrypha. They are not in the same world with the Book of Daniel, nor do they move on the same plane with Daniel. Yet Daniel, according to the rationalistic critics, is one of them!

2. If, in our wildest, evil imagination, we grant that the Book of Daniel belongs to The Pseudepigrapha, then who is the ancient worthy named "Daniel" under whose name the forgery is pawned off? Searching through the Bible we find a certain Daniel in I Chronicles 3:1, the son of David and Abigail. But nothing else is known of him. So he will not do. Continuing to search through the Bible, we find a certain Daniel in Ezra 8:2 and in Nehemiah 10:6, one among the many thousands of returning exiles. But nothing else is known of him. So he will not do. Then we come to a Daniel named in Ezekiel 14:14, 20; 28:3. This is he! The critics have found the ancient worthy under whose name the forgery called "The Book of Daniel" was written. Here is a man famous for wisdom, a Biblical hero like Adam and Enoch and Abraham. But when the infidel critics seek to present this "Daniel" of Ezekiel 14:14, 20; 28:3 as a hero revered and loved through the centuries,

they have to admit that absolutely nothing is known about him! He is completely *unknown!*

3. In their frantic efforts to identify the Daniel of Ezekiel 14 and 28 as an ancient worthy whose name could be used for a Pseudepigraphon, modern rationalistic critics have seized upon a heathen hero uncovered in the archaeological diggings at Ras Shamra in Northern Syria. About 1930 archaeologists who were sifting through the remains of ancient Ugarit (modern Ras Shamra) discovered clay tablets recounting the legend of Aqhat. The father of this Aqhat was a Canaanite by the name of Dan'el who lived about 1400 B.C. This Dan'el is presented in their Ugaritic literature as being wise and just in his judgment of the fatherless and the widows. In this way he became a legend and thus came to be named by Ezekiel in 14:14, 20 along with Noah and Job.

But look! As this Ugaritic literature is more closely searched, several things about this Dan'el come to light. First, he prays to Baal. He eats his meal in the house of Baal. Second, he sets up a stele of his ancestral gods in a shrine. He offers oblations to these heathen gods. Third, this Dan'el curses in revenge and mourns as one who does not have hope in the living God. Is it possible, is it imaginable, that the prophet Ezekiel held up this man before the Jews as an epitome of righteous dedication to Jehovah? Is this the ancient worthy a spurious Jewish writer chose for his forgery? To what lengths will these modern, rationalistic critics go to dishonor and discredit the Book of Daniel!

4. We cannot help but make one other comment about the critics' identification of the Daniel of the Bible. They say the real author was "an unknown holy and pious Jew" who wrote his pseudepigraphon about 165 B.C. But just how "holy" and "pious" was the man who would pawn off such history as real prophecy? According to the critics, the whole writing is fiction, romance, imagination. Yet the author of the Book of Daniel would have us believe that his word is prophetic, the very unveiling of the future by

the infinite foreknowledge of God. Such a deception negates the ideas of "holy" and "pious." The author is either what he said he was or else he is a liar and a deceiver. Semantics and nomenclature do not place in the same world the "liar" and "the deceiver" with "the holy" and "the pious." The critics are going to have to retract their language.

III. The Real Daniel of the Bible

As there was a real Enoch, a real Moses, a real Isaiah, so there was a real Daniel somewhere, sometime. Who was he and when did he write? The critics say that the existence of the Pseudepigrapha, these false apocalypses, carry with them the certainty that the Book of Daniel was also one of them and that the author who wrote under the name of "Daniel" was also one of these faceless, anonymous, unknown apocalyptic writers. But some most pertinent observations are to be made about such a dramatic and unusual conclusion. That there are spurious apocalypses no more proves that all apocalypses are spurious than that there are spurious gospels and epistles prove that none are genuine. That there is counterfeit money does not prove that none is genuine. False statements in II Maccabees do not prove that I Maccabees is not genuine. Spurious Acts of the Apostles do not prove that Luke's Acts of the Apostles is not true. So, false apocalypses, in fact, the whole pseudepigrapha, do not prove that there are no genuine apocalypses. Surely, there must have been a beginning, a first apocalypse at some time, if ever. Daniel is the *first* and genuine apocalypse. The Pseudepigrapha are but poor and false imitations and counterfeits of the real.

In the Book of Daniel we discover genuine, historical facts drawn from independent sources. In the Book of Daniel we possess a masterpiece, a marvel of literature, a display of super-human wisdom. The centuries bear witness to the truth of its prophecies. If the Book of Daniel is a Pseudepigraphon of the Maccabean period, we are baffled by the phenomena displayed in the volume. But if it is a genuine work of the early Persian period, all is clear enough. The fact is, the critics who do not believe in miracles have, themselves, constituted a theory which requires us to believe a miracle far beyond these we read in the Book, itself; namely, that an unknown Jew, living in 165 B.C., four hundred years after the events described, could have fabricated such a marvel of history and prophecy.

Like the story told in the gospels, the narrative in the Book of Daniel is simple and straightforward. The simplicity of truth is through it all. The whole atmosphere of the writing is faithful to the historical times in which it records its story. The amazing details, confirmed by tablets and inscriptions, bricks and historical records, all confirm the identity of the author as the Daniel of the captivity.

Who was the Daniel who wrote the Book called by his name in the Bible?

1. He was a man in the court of princes, in high estate and governmental service in Babylon under Nebuchadnezzar, Belshazzar and Cyrus. Yet faithful to God though a captive hero.

2. He was a man of tremendous spiritual courage. Witness his judgment upon King Belshazzar in Daniel 5:22-28. Witness his fearless spiritual commitments as recorded in Daniel 6:10.

3. He was a man whom money and power could not corrupt. Read Daniel 5:17.

4. He was a man of prayer and intercession. Read Daniel 9:17a, 18, 19.

5. He was a man greatly beloved by God and man. Look at Daniel 9:23; 10:11, 19.

6. He was a man of great personal hope and confidence in the future. Read again Daniel 2:44, 45; 6:16, 22; 12:12, 13.

7. He was a man God used to color the prophetic revelation of the centuries that followed him. Zechariah, Jesus, Paul and John reflect the wisdom God bestowed upon "the prophet Daniel."

This is the real Daniel of the Bible.

Chapter V

DANIEL IN THE EYES OF HIS CONTEMPORARIES

. . . O Daniel, a man greatly beloved . . .
Daniel 10:11

We are not without references and resources to look upon the prophet-statesman Daniel as he appeared in the eyes of those who lived in his own day. Both in the court of the king and among the exiles who lived in the land, Daniel is seen and described with intimate perspective. It shall be the purpose of this chapter, therefore, to behold the prophet as he served the state and as he walked in and out before the people of his own nativity.

I. Daniel in the Eyes of the Prophet Ezekiel

Three times does Ezekiel, the younger contemporary of Daniel, mention the prophet-statesman. Ezekiel refers to Daniel in Ezekiel 14:14, 14:20, and 28:23.

1. The attack of the critics against the identification of the Daniel mentioned by Ezekiel and the Daniel of the Book in the Bible as being the same man is most fierce and most destructive. The critics avow that it is unthinkable and unimaginable that Daniel, a contemporary of Ezekiel, could have been named between the ancient patriarchs Noah and Job, as Ezekiel does in Ezekiel 14:14: "Though these three men, Noah, Daniel, and Job, were in it, they should deliver but their own souls by their righteousness, saith the Lord God," and in Ezekiel 14:20: "Though Noah, Daniel, and

Job, were in it, as I live, saith the Lord God, they shall deliver neither son nor daughter; they shall but deliver their own souls by their righteousness."

For one thing, the critics avow that Daniel was too young to have arrived at such a stature of wisdom and holiness in the days of the prophet Ezekiel. They avow this, even though Daniel, at the time Ezekiel uttered these prophecies, was middle-aged. In casting about for some kind of a hero named Daniel that Ezekiel must have referred to, the critics have hit upon the Dan'el of Ugarit. In the previous chapter we have discussed this mythological Canaanitish hero Dan'el of the Aqhat epic of Ras Shamra. He was a heathen idol worshiper, and it is unthinkable that the prophet of Jehovah, Ezekiel, would have placed him alongside righteous Noah and Job. The only Daniel that we know that Ezekiel could refer to is this Daniel of the Book who bears his name in the Bible. There is no other.

2. For a moment let us look more closely at the prophet Ezekiel. He was a young priest taken captive by the armies of Nebuchadnezzar in 598 B.C., eleven years before the final invasion and destruction of Jerusalem in 587 B.C. He was chosen, as Daniel was in his day of the captivity of 605 B.C., because of his superior gifts. Neither II Kings 24:10-16, nor any other book (as Jeremiah, Ezekiel, or Daniel) mentions any priests among those who were carried away captive with King Jehoiachin. He was probably chosen to be removed to Babylon because of his reputation, his gifts, and his other sterling qualities. This superior and gifted type of personality Nebuchadnezzar greatly desired for the building of his kingdom in Babylonia.

There is no hint in the Scriptures of Ezekiel's age when he was taken captive. Josephus (Ant. X, 7,3) says he was a boy when he was removed to Babylon. This is probably a guess. Ezekiel could have been thirty years old when he was exiled in the land of the Euphrates.

Ezekiel was a younger contemporary of Jeremiah. As Jeremiah was the great prophetic figure in Judah and Jerusalem during those tragic days of Nebuchadnezzar's invasions, so Ezekiel was the great prophetic figure in Babylon during the exile. As the one delivered God's message in the Holy Land, so the other delivered God's Word in a foreign land.

In Babylon Ezekiel settled down with his fellow countrymen in a community named Tel-abib, along the canal Chebar, a short distance southeast of Babylon (Ezekiel 3:15). The river Chebar is now known from cuneiform inscriptions to be the Babylonian canal Kabar in central Babylonia, a barge traffic artery running between Babylon and the city of Nippur, located sixty miles southeast of the capital. The same word to denote both a river and a canal was employed by the Babylonians. So when we read "the river Chebar" we are actually referring to "the canal Chebar." Telabib has now been identified as the Babylonian Tel-abubi, which means "mound of the deluge." Names compounded with the syllable "Tel" were common in Babylonia.

Five years after Ezekiel's departure from Jerusalem he saw the remarkable vision recorded in Ezekiel, Chapter 1. After this he received a commission to bring God's message to the rebellious house of Israel recorded in Chapter 2. He ate the scroll described in Chapter 3, after which he went to sit with the captives (Ezekiel 3:12, 15), and thus he began his prophetic ministry.

In his prophetic deliverances he thus speaks of Daniel in Ezekiel 14:14, 20; 28:3. Could it be, could it have been, that this Ezekiel could have placed his contemporary Daniel along with the ancient heroes of Noah and Job? To the critics, as I have pointed out, such a thing is unimaginable and unthinkable.

3. When we review this possibility of Ezekiel's exalted appraisal of Daniel we are immediately confronted with the avowal of the unbeliever that Daniel was too young for Ezekiel even to have known, much less to have thus referred to him. The truth is that Daniel had ample time to establish himself and his great reputation in Babylon by the time of

Ezekiel's prophecies. Ezekiel began his ministry some thirteen or fourteen years after Daniel's exile. Daniel must have been thirty-five or forty years of age when Ezekiel referred to him in his prophecies.

We must not forget that some of the greatest figures of all time did their life's work before they reached their middle thirties. At thirty-four years of age Napoleon was emperor of Europe's greatest empire and the foremost figure in the world of his day. At thirty-three years of age Alexander the Great was dead, having conquered the whole civilized earth. And it is certainly not forgotten that at thirty-three years of age Jesus was crucified and died, having left upon the memory of mankind the incomparably greatest life that has ever been lived.

When Ezekiel wrote these prophecies, probably in 572 B.C., Daniel was in the prime of his power and in the zenith of his fame and could have been nearly fifty years of age. It just remains for us to consider whether or not such a man could have been so revered in the hearts of the people and in the judgment of the prophet Ezekiel and dear to the heart of God that he could have been named along with the ancient heroes Noah and Job. Let us look at this further as Daniel appeared before the eyes of his fellow countrymen.

II. Daniel in the Eyes of His Fellow Exiles

It is easy for us, both from our study of the Jewish people in general and, also, from our careful perusal of the Book of Daniel, to judge the stature of this prophet statesman in the eyes of his own people. To follow this appraisal is to bring to our hearts one of the most poignant presentations in all Biblical history.

1. The Jews in exile were permitted to form colonies in which their life and customs were meticulously continued. They took to heart the counsel of Jeremiah in Jeremiah 29:5, 10, 28 and Jeremiah 25:11, 12 and prepared for an exile of seventy years. This meant that few of those who were carried captive to Babylon could ever expect to return to their

native land and to the holy city of Jerusalem. There is a sadness in their slave life that is almost inexpressible. The Holy Spirit of God has given us a poignant expression of the tragic life of these exiles in a song that they left behind. Let us read again Psalm 137:1-9:

> By the rivers of Babylon, there we sat down, yea, we wept, when we remembered Zion.
>
> We hanged our harps upon the willows in the midst thereof.
>
> For there they that carried us away captive required of us a song; and they that wasted us required of us mirth, saying, Sing us one of the songs of Zion.
>
> How shall we sing the Lord's song in a strange land?
>
> If I forget thee, O Jerusalem, let my right hand forget her cunning.
>
> If I do not remember thee, let my tongue cleave to the roof of my mouth; if I prefer not Jerusalem above my chief joy.
>
> Remember, O Lord, the children of Edom in the day of Jerusalem; who said, Rase it, rase it, even to the foundation thereof.
>
> O daughter of Babylon, who are to be destroyed; happy shall he be, that rewardeth thee as thou hast served us.
>
> Happy shall he be, that taketh and dasheth thy little ones against the stones.

As we read these verses, we can literally feel the hot teardrops fall from their eyes to the ground.

2. This sadness of exile was compounded ten thousand times when the captives looked upon what their sins had done to the flower of their own youth. Their compassion for the seed royal must have reached a height and a depth unknown to us. The prophet Isaiah had delivered a message from God many, many years before this time, in which he had said that the seed of the kings of Judah would be made eunuchs in the courts of the king of Babylon. "Behold, the days come, that all that is in thine house, and that which the fathers have laid up in store until this day,

shall be carried to Babylon: nothing shall be left, saith the Lord. And of thy sons that shall issue from thee, which thou shalt beget, shall they take away; and they shall be eunuchs in the palace of the king of Babylon" (Isaiah 39: 6, 7).

Daniel is a victim of this judgment of God upon the sins of the people. He was of princely extraction, the seed royal. Born to rule, he was bred in the expectation of a scepter. He never dreamed of slavery to a heathen monarch in a foreign land. Yet, in the life of this youth the prophecy of Isaiah and the judgment of God, sadly and tragically, came to pass. He was made a eunuch in the court of the king of Babylon. He was a dry tree. He was an emasculated man with no hope of family or issue or posterity.

The visitation of wrath upon Judah and Jerusalem was fierce and terrible beyond anything the nation had ever experienced. In such a destruction the innocent are always compelled to suffer with the guilty. It is thus with all war and in all battles. The fierceness of the strife sweeps along with it the agony of the poor and the innocent. The sins of the fathers are visited upon the children. We cannot but be reminded of the plaintive cry of Elizabeth Barrett Browning as she witnessed the personal suffering of the children of England as they toiled in the sweatshops of factory slavery in England.

> Do you hear the children
> weeping, O my brothers;
> Ere the sorrow comes
> with years?
>
> They are leaning their young
> heads against their mothers,
> And that cannot stop
> their tears.
>
> The young lambs are
> bleating in the meadows;
> The young birds are
> chirping in the nest;

The young fawns are
  playing with the shadows,
The young flowers are
  bending toward the west.

But the young, young
  children, O my brothers!
They are weeping bitterly,
  in the playtime of the others,
In the country of the free.

Personal grief and deepest sorrow must have smote the very souls of the exiles, as they looked upon their young prince Daniel. "This," they must have said, "is what our sins have done."

3. The purity of the character of Daniel could not but have made a deep and everlasting impression upon the minds of the Jewish exiles. We know more of Daniel himself than about most of the other prophets of the Bible. In this knowledge of the man personally we can compare him with our knowledge of Isaiah and Jeremiah. Daniel was taken captive in his youth. He lived through the whole period of the captivity of seventy years. Throughout that long, long vista of time he was in the public gaze, regardless of the changes of political life. Anyone who is acquainted with public life at all could not but be cognizant of the fierce glare of the corporate gaze as they sift through every thought, every word, every act, every deed, every choice, every decision of a public servant. Yet, after three-quarters of a century of this public exhibition, the verdict concerning Daniel is clearly and unmistakably voiced by the provincial presidents who were serving under king Darius, as recorded in Daniel 6:4, 5. "Then the presidents and princes sought to find occasion against Daniel concerning the kingdom; but they could find none occasion nor fault; forasmuch as he was faithful, neither was there any error or fault found in him. Then said these men, We shall not find any occasion against this Daniel, except we find it against him concerning the law of his God."

The spotless character and the flawless life of Daniel can be beautifully compared with the life of Joseph and the life of Jonathan. There was no break in his moral constitution. Though in high office and in public life, his character was never impeached. He talked with angels. He had visions of God. The very words of the Almighty were spoken in his hearing. His tremendous reputation is referred to as in years later the author of Hebrews mentions him among the heroes of faith (Hebrews 11:33).

4. Daniel was "greatly beloved." This is stated three different times, as in Daniel 9:23: "At the beginning of thy supplications the commandment came forth, and I am come to shew thee; for thou art greatly beloved: therefore understand the matter, and consider the vision." And in Daniel 10:11: "And he said unto me, O Daniel, a man greatly beloved, understand the words that I speak unto thee, and stand upright: for unto thee am I now sent." And again in Daniel 10:19: "O man greatly beloved, fear not: peace be unto thee, be strong, yea, be strong."

As "the beloved disciple" John was dear to the heart of Jesus, so the beloved statesman-prophet Daniel was dear to the heart of Jehovah. He was loved by God; he was loved by men; and particularly and especially he was loved by his fellow exiles in Babylon. Ezekiel, himself, could not have escaped this marvelous reverence and holy gratitude for the beloved Daniel.

His fidelity to the faith of his fathers is clearly seen in the choice that he made, as recorded in Daniel 1:8: "But Daniel purposed in his heart that he would not defile himself with the portion of the king's meat, nor with the wine which he drank: therefore he requested of the prince of the eunuchs that he might not defile himself."

His love for his people and his country is especially prominent as we read of his faithful habits of prayer and the substance of his intercessions, as recorded in Daniel 6:10: "Now when Daniel knew that the writing was signed, he went into his house; and his windows being open in his chamber toward Jerusalem, he kneeled upon his knees three times a day, and prayed, and gave thanks before his God, as he did aforetime."

Such a devotion could not have been lost upon the people of the exile nor upon their great prophet, Ezekiel.

5. Daniel's exalted place at court possibly meant more to the slaves of Judah than any other one historical fact of the age. He was their representative and their advocate. They were so enslaved, so lost, so subject to every whim of the king, but he was in a position of dazzling splendor and influence, second only to that of the great monarch himself. Daniel's fame and power, great as it was, could not have failed to have loomed even greater still in the eyes of the humble exiles on the river Chebar, among whom Ezekiel lived and prophesied. Neither Noah nor Job would have possessed so large a place in their hearts and in the hopes of the people. The name of their great patron Daniel must have been on every lip. His power was their security against excessive oppression. His influence gave them added hope against the day of their return to the land of their fathers. The greatness of Daniel in the court of the king, his love for his people and the faith of his fathers, the purity of his character, the nobility of his life, all conspired to make him God's greatest man in the eyes of his people. To number him and to name him with Noah and Joseph was psychologically possible and easily explicable in the day in which he lived.

6. Ezekiel 28:3 refers to Daniel's reputation for wisdom: "Behold, thou art wiser than Daniel; there is no secret that they can hide from thee." Daniel gained this reputation in a court that was characterized by unfailing ambition to make itself known over the world as the most gifted and the most knowledgeable of all the generations in human history. The Chaldean Magi thus came to be the most famous for wisdom in the ancient civilized world. This reputation continued through the centuries, even down to the life of Christ. The story of the birth of Jesus includes, in the second chapter of Matthew, a glorious narrative of the coming of these Magi

from the far east to worship Him who had been born king of the Jews.

It is almost startling to remember that in the days of Ezekiel's prophecies Daniel had been the chief of these Magi for more than a score of years. In wisdom, as well as in statecraft, he continued to be the foremost figure in the court of Babylon for three-quarters of a century. And if we know anything about human nature at all, we can know this: that his story of triumph would have lost nothing in its telling among his people.

As they spoke one to another then of the marvelous grace of God upon him, so his reputation for wisdom and holiness, for courage and devotion unto death, continued through the centuries that followed. In I Maccabees old Mattathias exhorted his sons to be faithful unto death, urging upon them the example of the prophet Daniel.

Among the heroes of faith in the 11th Chapter of Hebrews the author speaks of that one who was able under God to stop the mouths of lions. And thus it has continued to the present day. The phrase, "Dare to be a Daniel," is a common one heard in the pulpits of the land and in exhortations to our young people. For Daniel thus to be numbered among the heroes of ancient times, even in the company of Noah and Job, is not out of order, nor is it a psychological impossibility. The prophet-statesman was thus exalted, loved and honored in his own day, as he is in our day, and as he has been through the centuries since he graced the court of the king of Babylon.

Chapter VI

THE LANGUAGE OF GOD

Then spake the Chaldeans to the king in Syriac . . .
Daniel 2:4

During these many years that I have studied and prepared messages to deliver to our people, there has never been a study that has engrossed me more deeply or that has interested me more unwearingly than this study concerning the languages we find in God's Holy Word. The effort has been one of the most rewarding I have ever dedicated to God. So much have I learned and what I have learned is so meaningful to my understanding of the Bible. Let us, therefore, reverently look at these inspired words that are found in the Holy Scriptures and let us learn from whence they came.

I. The Phenomenon of Language We Find in the Bible

Once I supposed that there were only two languages used by the inspired men who wrote the Bible. One was Hebrew, in which the Old Testament is written; the other was Greek, in which the New Testament is written. But there is another language found in the Bible, and that language is the Aramaic embedded in the Old Testament. Aramaic passages occur in the Old Testament Hebrew in four places.

1. Genesis 31:47. "And Laban called it Jegar-sahadutha: but Jacob called it Galeed."

The two words "Jegar-sahadutha" translate a Hebrew

toponym into Aramaic, the language of Laban. Both the Aramaic and the Hebrew mean "a heap of witness." In Hebrew it is "Galeed." In Aramaic it is "Jegar-sahadutha."

2. Jeremiah 10:11. "Thus shall ye say unto them, The gods that have not made the heavens and the earth, even they shall perish from the earth, and from under these heavens."

This one sentence in a unique phenomenon in itself. There is no Hebrew original. There is only this Aramaic. It has been suggested that the Hebrew original for this one verse was lost and the hiatus was filled in with this Aramaic. Such a suggestion, of course, is possible. It is most probable, however, that Jeremiah gives the answer his people were to say to their conquerors when they were invited to worship their heathen gods, and Jeremiah gave the answer in Aramaic, the language of the heathen people who would be thus speaking. In any event, the only original language we have for Jeremiah 10:11 is in Aramaic.

3. Ezra 4:8–6:18; 7:12-26. These two passages comprise about one-third of the Book of Ezra. The paragraphs include the official documents concerning the restoration of the Temple in Jerusalem. Since the original documents were written in Aramaic, the reproduction of their words is in the original language as they were copied by the scribe, Ezra.

4. Daniel 2:4–7:28. This long and extended passage comprises one-half of the Book of Daniel. Ezra was brought up in Babylon. Daniel was taken there when a young man. To both of them, therefore, Aramaic was almost as well known as their native Hebrew tongue. Both drop into Aramaic upon the slightest suggestion: Ezra, upon quoting an Aramaic letter; Daniel, upon quoting the frightened Chaldeans. Both men are equally at home in one language as well as the other.

All of this leads us to a most important and a most interesting question. What is this Aramaic language and where did it come from? Who are these Arameans?

II. The History of the Arameans

In Genesis 10:22 we are told that one of the sons of Shem was Aram. He is named in Matthew 1:3 and in Luke 3:33. The Semitic descendants of Aram were called Arameans. The Greeks called the Arameans "Syrians," an abbreviation of Assyrians. The Greeks met these people as subjects of the vast Assyrian Empire and so called them by the name of their conquerors and rulers. Actually, the Arameans were an altogether different people from the Assyrians. In our English Bibles the Hebrew word for "Aramean" is usually translated "Syrian."

These Semitic people were the most widely distributed of the descendants of Shem. They were scattered throughout the fertile crescent, that vast region of western Asia extending from the mountains of Media, through the Mesopotamian Valley, through Eastern Asia Minor, down through Syria and Palestine and reaching to the Nile Valley. Their language became the speech of Mesopotamia, of Syria, of Palestine, and continued through the centuries until it was supplanted by Arabic after the Mohammedan Conquest in the seventh century, A.D. As a whole, the Arameans never formed a political national unit. This, in itself, is a most remarkable thing, because usually a people who have such extensive repercussions in civilization are almost always gathered together in some tremendous national organization. It was not so with the Arameans. Their effect upon civilization was tremendous and extensive in the extreme, yet they were never, as a whole, united in any national unit.

The Old Testament distinguishes several Aramean groups. Among them are these:

1. Aram Naharaim, "Aram of the two rivers," that is, the Aram between the Euphrates and the Tigris Rivers. The word "Aram Naharaim" is translated in the King James Version of the Bible "Mesopotamia" in Genesis 24:10; Deuteronomy 23:4; Judges 3:8, 10; and in I Chronicles 19:6. The word, however, is spelled out as such in the title of Psalm 60.

Sometimes this same land and its people are called Paddan-Aram (Genesis 25:20; 28:2, 5-7; 31:18; 33:18; 35:9, 26; 46:15). This Paddan-Aram is the home of Laban and Rebecca, the children of Bethuel, the son of Nahor, which Nahor was the brother of Abraham.

2. Aram Damascus. In the Bible Damascus was often simply called Aram because it was the section of the people best known to Israel. From this intimate acquaintance on the part of the Hebrew people we sometimes find in the Scriptures the word Aram used by the people of Israel for ancient Syria. In fact, as the people spoke in the vernacular of their everyday conversation, their use of the word Aram would refer to ancient Syria.

3. Aram Zobah. During the days of Saul and David in the eleventh century B.C., the most powerful realm in Syria was this Aram Zobah (I Samuel 14:47; II Samuel 8:3; 10: 6, 8). The district lay between Hamath, to its north, and Damascus, to its south, and at its height its influence reached these cities.

The Arameans were shepherds and traders. They had the instinct of travel and commerce. Even as shepherds, they were not like the Bedouin-Arams, for they kept their flocks and herds mainly for sale in the markets of the cities near where they were usually found. As traders they were for land traffic what the Phoenicians were on the sea. They controlled the business and commerce of western Asia throughout successive kingdoms and empires. Their great trading center in upper Mesopotamia was Haran, in the district of Paddan-Aram, one of the greatest trading cities of the ancient East. (You remember that Abraham went from Ur of Chaldea to Haran, Genesis 11:31.) Their great trading center in northeast Palestine was Damascus, the greatest city and the capital of the greatest state ever controlled by the Arameans.

The unifying process through which the whole of western Asia passed under the domination of Assyria, Neo-Babylonian and Persian Empires was materially hastened by the presence of the ubiquitous Arameans. Palestine, itself, gradually became Aramean in speech and in methods of trade and commerce.

III. The Language of the Arameans

The language of these ubiquitous traders became the language of commerce and eventually the language of the state. This amazing development can be seen in the story of the successive empires that ruled in that ancient part of the world.

1. *Assyria.* Along with the Arameans already in Assyria, Assyrian conquerors took many other Arameans, as from Damascus, and settled them in their extensive lands in the upper Mesopotamian Valley. The language of these Arameans conquered the Assyrians. Aramaic became the language of diplomatic communication between Assyria and the provinces of western Asia. For example, read the story of the siege of Jerusalem recounted in II Kings 18:17-37. Aramaic is herein easily seen as the international language in the days of Sennacherib. It was a language understood by the high Assyrian and Jewish officials but not understood by the common people of Jerusalem.

The Semitic languages of Hebrew and Aramaic have the same qualities of likeness and difference as can be found in the Romance languages of French and Italian, or the Teutonic languages of Anglo-Saxon-English and German. As a Frenchman cannot understand an Italian, or as an Englishman cannot understand a German, so the people of Jerusalem who spoke Hebrew could not understand the Aramaic of the Assyrian officials; but, being an international language, the high officials of the Jerusalem government could readily understand the diplomatic language of the officers of the Assyrian army. Abraham doubtless spoke the Aramaic of ancient Mesopotamia, but when he came to Palestine, he and his family and his descendants gradually changed to speak the language of Canaanitic-Hebrew.

2. *Babylonia.* Aramaic was the official language of the Babylonian Empire. It was the predominant language spoken by the heterogenous population of the great metropolis, Babylon. For example, archaeologists, digging in the ruins of Babylon, have found business contracts written in Babylonian cuneiform, yet on the backs of the contracts are written labels in Aramaic for quick reference by the clerks in the office. This plainly shows that however polyglot the mixture of population might be in the ancient capital of the Babylonian Empire, the one common denominator in which all would share was the use of the Aramaic language.

3. *Persia.* The language of diplomacy in the Persian Empire and the means of communication between the Persian rulers and the polyglot nations they ruled was Aramaic. Most probably Ezra 4:11-22; 5:7-17; 6:3-12; 7:11-26 are actually copies of original texts kept in Persian archives. The one medium of communication in their far flung administration open to the Persian kings and their officials was this dominant spoken language of Aramaic. As the tongue was used in court, in commerce, in army life, it became known as official or imperial Aramaic, the language of governmental officials. Aramaic became the "lingua franca" of nearer Asia, as English or French is today.

4. *The Jewish Exiles.* During the exile a change took place in the speech habits of the Jews. In pre-exilic days their language was Hebrew. When the exiles returned to the land of Palestine, after the Babylonian Captivity, they still continued to speak Hebrew. For example, the Books of Haggai, Zechariah and Malachi are written in Hebrew. But beside this Biblical Hebrew there was something other added. During the exile the Jews learned to speak Aramaic as a means of communication with their non-Jewish neighbors. When they returned to Jerusalem, they not only carried this Aramaic language with them, but they also found it there in the homeland. For example, in Nehemiah 8:8, when Ezra read the law, it was necessary to give an interpretation of the meaning of the written text. This interpre-

tation was probably in Aramaic. As time continued, a most astonishing and remarkable thing happened in Palestine with the Jews who returned to the homeland. That remarkable thing is this: The Aramaic language altogether displaced the Hebrew as the spoken and written language of the people. Just when the Hebrew of Palestine was displaced by the Aramaic of the Arameans, we cannot determine. It gradually came to pass in this post-exilic period. Originally there were three great north Semitic dialects: Assyrian-Babylonian, Canaanitic-Hebrew, and Aramean. The latter altogether displaced the other two as a living speech.

Some of the repercussions of this use of the Aramaic language can be easily followed in Old Testament history.

1. As the Jewish people became an Aramaic speaking people, the Old Testament Hebrew Scripture had to be translated into Aramaic. These translations are called Targums. The Hebrew verses are explained in Aramaic for all of the people to understand.

2. All the Hebrew Bibles were copies in Aramaic script using the Aramaic alphabet. Only the Samaritan community preserved the old Hebrew script. All our Hebrew Bibles, without exception, are written in Aramaic script and not in ancient Hebrew script. The words are Hebrew, but the alphabet that is used in Aramaic. The truth of the matter is that a great many of the languages of the ancient world received their alphabet from the Arameans.

3. The tremendous religious works of the Hebrews known to us as the Talmuds are written in Aramaic. The Babylonian Talmud is written in Babylonia-Aramaic, and the Palestinian Talmud is written in Palestinian-Aramaic. The Talmuds are not written in Hebrew. They are written in Aramaic.

4. The spoken language of Christ was Aramaic. His original Aramaic words are sometimes kept in the gospel narrative, such as can be seen in Mark 5:41, "Talitha cumi;" Mark 7:34, "Ephphatha;" Mark 15:34, "Eloi, Eloi, lama sabachthani" and Mark 14:36, "Abba." Aramaic words are

also used in the Epistles of Paul the Apostle. The Apostle was doubtless as familiar with Aramaic as he was with Hebrew or Greek. Paul uses an Aramaic word in Romans 8:15, and again in I Corinthians 16:22. It could well have been that when Christians all over the Roman Empire bade one another farewell, they used the Aramaic "maranatha" in the same way that we would use the English word "good-by." In the story of Christian missionary conquest a great deal of early Christian literature was written in the Aramaic dialect known to us as Syriac.

IV. The Aramaic of the Book of Daniel

Daniel, like the Aramaic documents in Ezra, is half written in Imperial Aramaic, the official literary dialect which had currency in all parts of the near east. The Hebrew of Daniel is in the same style as that of Ezekiel, his fellow exile. The Aramaic of Daniel is like the court language spoken in the sixth century B.C.

We now consider what it means that these two languages, both Hebrew and Aramaic, are used in the Book of Daniel. There are many suggestions concerning the reason for this dual speech. We consider three of these suggestions.

1. There are those who say that the two languages show that there are two or more different authors who composed the Book of Daniel. This suggestion might be considered if the parts differed also in style, content and use of words, but this is not true at all. Daniel 2:4, where the Aramaic begins, is part of a coherent narrative with Daniel 2:5. Reading the story in English, one would never know that there is a change of language from Hebrew to Aramaic. Chapter 7 (written in Aramaic) belongs with Chapter 8 (written in Hebrew). There is a general similarity in style, expression and idiom between the Hebrew and Aramaic sections. Whoever wrote one part also wrote the other part. The author of the Aramaic sections is also the author of the Hebrew sections.

Nor can the Book be divided between the historical section, Chapters 1 through 6, and the prophetic section, Chapters 7 through 12. There is a marked parallelism between Chapter 2 in the historical section and Chapter 7 in the prophetical section. The author of each section is the same author. One man wrote them all.

2. The suggestion is made that there was a lacuna, a gap, a hiatus in the original Hebrew (or Aramaic) manuscript and it was filled in at a later time from an Aramaic (or Hebrew) translation. If the original Book of Daniel was written in Hebrew, then the lacuna was filled in with Aramaic. If the original Book of Daniel was written in Aramaic, then the lacuna was filled in with Hebrew. This suggestion, of course, would be altogether possible were it not for this fact: From the very beginning Daniel seems to have been written this way, part of it Aramaic and part of it Hebrew. The Qumran fragments which have been discovered from the caves by the Dead Sea exhibit the same phenomena that we have in our present text of Daniel. Where we have Hebrew, those fragments have Hebrew, and where we have Aramaic, those fragments also have Aramaic.

3. It is my deeply and earnestly considered opinion that the two languages were used in reference to the two great divisions of people who were the subjects of the prophecies and of the histories recorded in the Book. What concerns the Jews especially was written in Hebrew (Daniel 1:1-23; 8:1–12:13). What concerns the Gentile Empires especially was written in their language. The Aramaic portion of the Book of Daniel is a revelation, especially of the times of the Gentiles.

Daniel was a minister in the government of the king. Aramaic was the language of diplomacy and commerce. The language was often on his lips. The section of his Book written in Aramaic was for the purpose of the wider outreach of his prophetic visions, thus making the Book available and meaningful to a larger number of leaders. The message of the Book is not only to the Hebrew people but also to the nations and empires and kingdoms and governments of the whole civilized world.

God has a message not only for His chosen family, but for all the peoples under the sun. God is not only a God of the Hebrews, but also He is the Lord of all creation. He reigns in the affairs of men, both pagan and Christian, both heathen and Hebrew, both saved and lost. There is one God who reigns in heaven, and there is one God who is sovereign over all the earth. The Book of Daniel, therefore, rises beyond the message of The Almighty to His chosen Hebrew people and reaches to the farthest ends of the earth. The language, therefore, of diplomacy, culture, commerce and conquest are used by Daniel as he makes the will of God known to civilized men of all the nations under the sun.

Chapter VII

GOD'S SOVEREIGN CHOICE OF NEBUCHADNEZZAR

> O thou king, the most high God gave Nebuchadnezzar thy father a kingdom, and majesty, and glory, and honour:
> And for the majesty that he gave him, all people, nations, and languages, trembled and feared before him: whom he would he slew; and whom he would he set up; and whom he would he put down.
> But when his heart was lifted up, and his mind hardened in pride, he was deposed from his kingly throne, and they took his glory from him:
> And he was driven from the sons of men; and his heart was made like the beasts, and his dwelling was with the wild asses: they fed him with grass like oxen, and body was wet with the dew of heaven; till he knew that the most high God ruled in the kingdom of men, and that he appointed over it whomsoever he will.
>
> Daniel 5:18-21

Someone has said that a great institution or business house is but the shadow of the family who heads it. In the same sense, it might be said that the Neo-Babylonian kingdom, which lasted from 625 B.C.-538 B.C., was the shadow of a single, gifted, illustrious Babylonian family, the family of Nebuchadnezzar.

No family mentioned in the Old Testament made a more meteoric flash across the horizon of history than the family of Nabopolassar and his son, Nebuchadnezzar. Nor did any family fade into obscurity more quickly than did this royal house in the degenerate Belshazzar. Strangely enough, this family of four known generations left behind it more material evidence of its day than any other family mentioned in the Bible. And still stranger, of the monarch Nebuchadnezzar more is said in the Bible than is said of any other heathen ruler. As we speak of King Nebuchadnezzar, we inevitably speak of the sovereign God who rules and presides over the nations of the earth and who brought the son of Nabopolassar to the helm of the golden empire of Babylonia. With this brief generalization as a background, we speak now of the sovereign choices of God in human history and particularly in the rise of the Neo-Babylonian Empire.

I. God Knows and Rules the Future

Glimpses of God's knowledge and sovereign purposes are sometimes made known to men.

1. In Isaiah 39:5-8 the Lord revealed, through Isaiah the prophet, to Hezekiah king of Judah, the future captivity of the children of Judah at the hands of the Babylonian king. The occasion of the prophecy was this: Merodach-baladan, king of the Chaldeans and king of Babylon, in about 702 B.C., sent letters and emissaries to Hezekiah ostensibly to congratulate him on his recovery from his serious illness. Actually, the Chaldean king sent his ambassadors to invite Hezekiah to join a conspiracy of nations against Assyria. Hezekiah was so overcome and so flattered by the visit of these highly favored foreign visitors that he displayed before their eyes all of his own personal possessions and all of the treasures of the house of God. Out of this psychopathic vanity the Lord sent Isaiah to announce to Hezekiah the coming Babylonian captivity. This is an instance of the knowledge and sovereign purposes of God made known to man many years before the judgment fell in recorded history.

2. Genesis 15:13, 16 recounts another instance of God's foreknowledge made known to man. In the fifteenth chap-

ter of Genesis, the Lord Jehovah reveals to Abraham that his seed will be captive in Egypt for four hundred years, "till the iniquity of the Amorite be full." God sees the end from the beginning and all history lies in the present tense before His infinite eyes. Once in a while, as here with Abraham, God will make known to one of His servants a piece of that vast history.

3. An unusual reference in the Bible to this kind of knowledge and purpose of God is presented in Romans 11:25: "For I would not, brethren, that ye should be ignorant of this mystery, lest ye should be wise in your own conceits; that blindness in part is happened to Israel, until the fulness of the Gentiles be come in." The word here translated "fulness" is the Greek word "pleroma." The word here refers to a definite number. The text avows that there is a certain number of Gentiles known to God who are going to be saved, and when the last one of that number is brought into the kingdom, then the Lord will turn to the final consummation of history, which will include the conversion of the Jewish nation (Romans 11:26-29).

To us, events happen a moment at a time, a day at a time, a week at a time. To us, the course of developing history is full of many surprises. None of this is true as history develops before God. He is never surprised. All history lies at once before Him and He sees every part of it, past, present and future, through all time. As in the ages past, so in the eternal future. Throughout this vast story God is working out His divine purposes.

The purpose of the Almighty is sometimes difficult for us to see. Sometimes centuries and even millenniums pass before we are able to plot the broad sweep of God's will. But His purposes never fail, and however the tides of history may be running for the moment, we can always be assured that God rules over the earth and that His will eventually and ultimately shall be done.

II. God Raises Up Men to Execute His Judgment

1. Look at Jeremiah 25:9; 27:6; 43:10. God calls the

heathen Nebuchadnezzar "my servant." This is a remarkable use of the Hebrew word "ebed," servant. It is the same word that the prophet and the psalmist applied to David (II Samuel 7:8; Psalm 78:70). It is the identical word applied to the future Messiah (Isaiah 42:1; 52:13). It is the exact word that God applied to Cyrus, king of Persia in Isaiah 44:28; 45:1, when the Lord refers to the Persian conqueror as "the shepherd" and "the anointed of Jehovah." This reveals to us that each ruler of the great empires of the earth was, in ways he did not realize, working out the purposes of God. His advent into human history to us may have seemed accidental or incidental or adventitious, but not so in the sovereign choices of The Almighty. Whether it is Nebuchadnezzar or Cyrus or some other pagan king, he rules and reigns in the sovereign purposes of God, and God uses these men to execute His judgments.

2. When God wills or purposes a thing, no man or group of men can countermand or interdict God's sovereign judgment. Jeremiah 27:2-11 records the fact that the prophet sent bonds and yokes to all the nations round about Judah, telling them to submit to the bondage of the king of Babylon, that their people might be spared and their nations might be blessed. The prophet declared that to rebel against the king of Babylon was to rebel against the will of God, for it was the Lord God who had delivered all of these nations into the hands of Nebuchadnezzar.

The twenty-eighth chapter of Jeremiah is one of the most dramatic in all the story of the people of God. Jeremiah wore a yoke around his neck as he walked up and down the streets of Jerusalem. This signified to the people God's message that the nation would be carried captive into Babylon. The false prophet, Hananiah, broke off the yoke from the neck of Jeremiah, declaring that God had liberated the people and that the power of Nebuchadnezzar over Jerusalem would soon come to an end. The falsity of this prediction was not only openly declared by the prophet Jeremiah to the people, but the message came also from the Lord that in that very year the false prophet, Hananiah, would certainly die. And he died in the seventh month of that same year. When God wills a judgment, there are no circumstances in history and no conspiracy of men on earth who can countermand that heavenly decree.

From one end of the Holy Scriptures to the other, these illustrations of God's sovereign judgments in the lives of nations and of men are dramatically presented. For example, in Isaiah 20:2 we read where the great prophet walked naked and barefoot three years through Jerusalem, declaring and illustrating the coming destructive power of Assyria and the helplessness of the surrounding nations against the predatory ravages of the winged bull of Asher. It was God who delivered these nations into the hands of Assyria and no man could prevent that judgment.

In the days of which we are speaking in the Book of Daniel, we read in Ezekiel 12:5-7 that the prophet dug through the wall of his own house. When he had made a large aperture, he carried out his own household stuff into the street, thus signifying the coming total captivity of Judah. What the Lord God was saying to the people in Jerusalem through His prophet Jeremiah, He was also declaring to His people in captivity in Babylon.

In Acts 21:11, we are told that the prophet Agabus took Paul's girdle and bound him, declaring that the owner of this girdle would be bound, imprisoned, and handed over to the Roman government if the apostle who owned the girdle persisted in going to Jerusalem. However Paul might love God, or however he might pray and be God's servant, yet the Lord God delivered him according to the word of the prophet into the hands of the pagan Romans. It is God who presides over the lives of men, and no one can escape the sovereign judgments of Him who sits above the circle of the earth.

3. However the personal characteristics of individual men, God uses them to execute His judgments. Nebuchadnezzar was a heathen idolater, as history in the Book of Daniel plainly describes. From Daniel 2:12; 3:19, we know

that he was revengeful, impatient, imperious, contumacious, autocratic. From Daniel 4:30, we know that he was vain and proud. But, however the personal characteristics of Nebuchadnezzar, God chose him and used him for the sovereign purposes The Almighty had ordained.

It is thus with the purposes of God throughout history. The prophet Isaiah lived in the days of the terrible scourge of the Assyrians under Sargon and Sennacherib. No more ruthless or merciless rulers ever cursed the earth than the bitter and hasty Assyrians. When Isaiah the prophet asked God the question why the people of the Lord were being delivered into the hands of Assyria, the Lord replied that the heathen king, with his more heathen army, was the rod of His anger and the staff of His indignation (Isaiah 10:5). God was using the merciless Assyrians to scourge the people of Israel and Judah. The same sovereign judgment of The Almighty was seen in the coming of the Babylonians to destroy Judah and Jerusalem. The prophet Habakkuk was sent of the Lord to announce to Judah their coming captivity to the king of Babylon (Habakkuk 1:6-10). But the announcement deeply troubled the prophet. However Judah may have sinned, yet they were not as vile as the blaspheming Babylonians. Why then, Habakkuk asks of God, would the Lord bring upon Judah such a heathen and idolatrous nation and deliver His own people into their hands? In Habakkuk 1:12 God gives the answer. The Lord avows that He has raised up the bitter Babylonians, that He has ordained them for judgment and established them for correction. They are the scourge in God's hand to bring judgment upon His own people.

This great and revealed fact in human history brings terror to my own soul as I view the modern course of our own beloved America. We may not be as vile, as atheistic, as merciless as the bitter and fanatical communist, but God may use that communist as the rod of His anger and the staff of His indignation to scourge America. Whether we live or die lies in the imponderables of Almighty God. If God, in His sovereign purpose, delivers us into the hands of our atheistic enemy, no army or navy or air fleet can deliver us from the judgment. Whether we live or die lies in the sovereign purposes of God. National strength expressed in armed might will not save us. It is God, and He alone, who can save us.

> Far-called, our navies melt away;
> On dune and headland sinks the fire:
> Lo, all our pomp of yesterday
> Is one with Nineveh and Tyre!
> Judge of the Nations, spare us yet,
> Lest we forget – lest we forget!
>
> *Rudyard Kipling*

III. The Invincible Conquests of Nebuchadnezzar

The life and far-flung conquests of Nebuchadnezzar, king of Babylon, were the subjects of many of the prophetic revelations of God. As foretold by Jeremiah 25:1 ff.; 27:1 ff.; 43:10, the nations around Judah were delivered into the hands of the conquering king. As foretold by Ezekiel 26:7; 29:19; 30:10, the city of Tyre and the nation of Egypt were made a part of his all-powerful domain. Finally, the beloved and holy city of Jerusalem, with its surrounding cities and country of Judah, were trampled under Nebuchadnezzar's feet. According to God's sovereign will, the civilized earth became a part of the golden kingdom of Babylon.

The unfolding story of Babylon is one of the most dramatically interesting to be found in all human history. In Genesis 10:10 we learn that Nimrod was the builder of the city of Babel (Babylon) on the plain of Shinar, and the city became the seat of idolatry. In the passing centuries the old Babylonian empire numbered among its great and famous kings the Amorite lawgiver, Hammurabi. This empire reached its zenith in the eighteenth century B.C. At this time the city of Babylon was made one of the wonder metropolises of the world. After the days of Hammurabi, however, the city and the nation went into eclipse. About a thousand years later the Neo-Babylonian kingdom rose to world dominion under another Semitic king, Nebuchadnezzar. So famous was this city of Babylon and so dazzling did Nebuchadnezzar make it, that it has become a type and a symbol of the great final city of the world, as we read in Revelation 17.

For centuries after the decay of the old Babylonian empire, the Assyrians ruled the Mesopotamian Valley and most of the civilized world around and beyond it. Their later capital was Nineveh, on the east bank of the Tigris River. The people were war-like and ruthless. Their armies were the scourge of humanity. When their last great ruler, Ashur-banipal, died in A.D. 625, his son was unable to keep the empire together. Nabopolassar, king of the Chaldeans, was Ashur-banipal's viceroy in Babylon. Upon the death of his master, the Assyrian monarch, Ashur-Banipal, Nabopolassar revolted and took all of Babylonia from Assyria. Cyaxares, king of the Medes, and a bitter enemy of Assyria, had been warring against the monarch at Nineveh for years. The two kings, Nabopolassar and Cyaxares, joined forces, and aided by the Sythians, they attacked the impregnable Assyrian capital, Nineveh, and, according to the prophecy of Nahum 2:1–3:19, the city fell in 612 B.C. So complete was the destruction of Nineveh, that the very site of the city was forgotten. The armies of Alexander the Great, centuries later, marched over it, absolutely oblivious to the fact that a great empire lay beneath their feet.

Upon the destruction of Nineveh, the remnant of the Assyrian army fled westward to Haran in northern Mesopotamia and made that metropolis their temporary capital. But, under the relentless pressure of Nabopolassar and his son, Nebuchadnezzar, it, too, fell to the Babylonians in 610 B.C. An attempt to retake Haran in 609 B.C. failed miserably. The Assyrian remnant then retreated to the far-famed city of Carchemish, on the banks of the Euphrates River, there with their Egyptian allies to make their final stand. In the great Battle of Carchemish, 605 B.C., the future of world empire was decided. The Battle of Carchemish was truly one of the most decisive battles of human history. As we shall see, the world power of Egypt was forever broken, never to rise again, and Babylon became the master of the civilized world.

It was this Battle of Carchemish that so greatly involved the ruler of Egypt. In the days of the Assyrian disasters at Nineveh and Haran, Pharaoh-Necho of Egypt saw an opportunity to gain control of the civilized world, if only the armies of Nabopolassar and Nebuchadnezzar could be stopped. This development in history set the stage for the last battle in the age old conflict for the control of Western Asia between the competing civilizations centering on the Nile and on the Tigris-Euphrates Rivers. While Nabopolassar was busy mopping up the remains of Assyria and consolidating his victories in the homeland, Necho entered Palestine, slew good king Josiah at Armageddon, then marched his vast army to Carchemish, where, with the Assyrians, he prepared to destroy the armed might of Babylonia. The aging and apparently ailing Nabopolassar met the challenge by sending his army under his son, Nebuchadnezzar, to battle the Egyptians. In the conflict that ensued, 605 B.C., Nebuchadnezzar was supremely triumphant. He dealt a crushing blow to the enemy, from which Egypt never recovered. God had said these things would come to pass, and come to pass they did, however the strength of Egypt and however vast the multitude of the army of Necho.

In the tremendous victory of Nebuchadnezzar at the Battle of Carchemish five things resulted.

(1) Assyria passed away forever. The great empire in this battle came to its ultimate and final end. She is never mentioned again as a moving force in human history.

(2) The back of Egypt was completely broken. She never rose again as a world power. Not to this day has Egypt been a decisive factor in the development of civilization, nor will she ever be. The Battle of Carchemish fought so long ago settled that forever.

(3) The magnificent city of Carchemish with its long and brilliant career was utterly destroyed by Nebuchadnezzar. It has lain buried under desert dust until modern excavations have brought its great monuments to the light of day. That such a tremendous city could have been so completely demolished and forgotten is a remarkable commentary on the fierceness of the onslaught of the Babylonian king. When he struck, he struck with the fury of The Almighty Himself.

(4) Judah became a vassal of Babylon, according to Isaiah 39:5-8. Of this servitude the prophets in the Old Testament Scripture speak so fully and so poignantly. No event that has ever happened in the history of God's people made so indelible a mark upon Judah as did the coming of Nebuchadnezzar.

(5) God brought Nebuchadnezzar to that chosen place wherein he was used in The Almighty's judicial dealing with His people. At the same time, he brought Daniel, His representative and prophet-statesman, to stand before the mighty monarch. For while Nebuchadnezzar was pursuing Necho and his army in their panic-stricken flight from Carchemish back through Palestine and Judah toward Egypt, word was brought to Nebuchadnezzar of the death of his father. He returned to Babylon to be crowned king and to consolidate his victories at home. But the king returned not alone. He carried back to Babylon a few of the choice members of the royal family of Judah to grace his court. It was not an extensive deportation; it was not an uprooting of the population; it was rather a matter of adding to the brilliance of his central empire. And of those chosen to be presented in the king's court at Babylon were four young men, named Daniel, Hananiah, Mishael, and Azariah. In it all God had an infinite purpose, and that sovereign purpose came to pass in God's way and in God's will. It is thus with the ways of The Almighty through all human history.

Chapter VIII

THE BABYLONIAN CAPTIVITY

> In the third year of the reign of Jehoiakim king of Judah came Nebuchadnezzar king of Babylon unto Jerusalem, and besieged it.
> And the Lord gave Jehoiakim king of Judah into his hands . . .
>
> Daniel 1:1, 2

As we read and meditate upon the Holy Scriptures we come to know God personally. We see God's ways and how God does. This is especially true as we follow the course of God's judgments upon Judah during the days of Daniel. The awesome truth witnessed here in God's Book makes my soul tremble and bows me on my knees with my face to the ground. As I read of the days of Daniel, it is as though I were reading the headlines of the newspapers in my own day. The same personal and national moral decay then is witnessed among us now. The same warnings from God to the people then are sounded now. The same pattern of national life then is developing now. And the same Almighty God who judged Judah then is judging our America and our world now.

Throughout this message on the Babylonian captivity three things are everlastingly apparent:

1. Before judgment falls, God warns His people again, and again, and again. Judgment never falls unexpectedly, unannouncedly. God sends His messengers before His face to state clearly and in trumpet tones what is to follow. The wages of sin is death: moral death, yes; spiritual death,

yes; but also personal, domestic and national death. No man, no family, no state and no nation can escape this judgment of Almighty God.

2. But even in the hammer blows of a falling judgment, God gives grace and time for repentance. God has no pleasure in the death of the wicked but pleads for the lost sinner and for the erring nation to turn and be saved (Ezekiel 18:23; 33:11). It is never too late to get right with God. If we repent (turn), God repents (turns). This can be poignantly and dramatically seen in Jonah 3:5-10. Facing impending disaster at the hands of God, Nineveh repented and clothed herself in sackcloth and in ashes. And God? "And God saw their works, that they turned from their evil ways; and God repented of the evil, that he had said that he would do unto them; and he did it not." Anytime, anywhere a man or a nation will turn to God, God will reward that repentance with mercy and forgiveness.

3. If judgment falls upon a sinning people, the purposes of God are not frustrated by a nation's failure. Out of the ashes of ruin, God's sovereign grace raises up another and a purified people to do His will in the earth. Every sorrow and tragedy that is visited upon a people, God bends toward His ultimate designs for goodness unto men. The kingdom of darkness cannot overwhelm the kingdom of God. The night cannot destroy the day. Satan cannot triumph over the Anointed Christ. Out of national disaster God raises some better thing for His people.

With these three eternal truths in mind, let us follow the story of the Babylonian captivity.

I. The Warnings of God to Judah

In the headlong plunge of Judah and the House of David toward the abyss of national disaster, God gave stern and terrible warning again and again of the tragic consequence of their sin. He did this in several ways.

1. God warned Judah by the calamitous, disastrous example of Israel's northern ten tribes. Gross idolatry was

made a way of life in the beginning of the separated kingdom by Jeroboam I. The worship of the golden calves at Bethel and at Dan were a national disgrace as well as an affront to Jehovah God. Nor would the nation heed the warnings of the prophets whom God sent to speak His message of judgment. Then the Almighty did something more than speaks words. God raised up the better and merciless Assyrian as "the rod of mine anger and the staff of mine indignation" (Isaiah 10:5). First came Tiglath-Pileser III (Pul) (745-727 B.C.) and placed Israel under heavy tribute II Kings 15:17-20). Then came Shalmeneser IV (727-722 B.C.) who besieged Samaria, the capital city of Israel. And finally, the end of the kingdom came to the advance of Sargon II (722-705 B.C.) who destroyed Samaria and carried away the ten tribes to Assyria (II Kings 17:6). When Israel sinned away her day of grace, nothing remained but final judgment. As Hosea cried, "Ephraim is joined to his idols, let him alone" (Hosea 4:17).

2. The Assyrian moved closer and closer to Judah (II Kings 16:7-9). The terrible visitation of national war because of the sins of the people moved nearer and nearer. When Sargon II fell in battle, he was followed by his son, Sennacherib (705-681 B.C.) who invaded Judah and shut up Jerusalem in a vise. Only because of the tears and prayers of good king Hezekiah and only because of the repentant intercessions of the prophet Isaiah did Judah find deliverance from the clutches of the army of Sennacherib. In answer to prayer God sent an angel to destroy one hundred and eighty-five thousand of Sennacherib's army in one dreadful night (Isaiah 37:36, 37). But even then, the unearthed clay cylinder called "The Annals of Sennacherib" contains boasts by the Assyrian king that he took captive out of Judah over two hundred thousand people.

But the nation did not repent before the increasingly heavy hand of God. Manasseh, the son and successor of Hezekiah, plunged the nation into more grievous idolatry than ever before. Esarhaddon (681-668 B.C.) moved against the little nation and compelled Manasseh to pay him tribute.

Esarhaddon was followed by his son Ashurbanipal (668-626 B.C.) who carried away the evil king Manesseh in chains to the capital of one of his provinces, Babylon (II Chronicles 33:9-11), but God is merciful and always forgiving. If we turn, God turns. If we confess our sins, God is faithful and just to forgive us our sins (I John 1:9). In his sorrow and captivity Manasseh turned to God and God, in turn, released him and restored him to his throne in Judah (II Chronicles 33:12, 13). But the seeds of iniquity sown by Manasseh brought forth a disastrous harvest among the people. Continuing in their descent of moral degradation, as Israel had done before them, the people of Judah also sinned away their day of grace. God refused to spare any longer. Judgment was beginning to fall (Jeremiah 15:4; II Kings 24:3).

3. Judah was warned not only by the scourge of the Assyrian armies but by her own prophets, also. A hundred fifty years before the final captivity, God sent Isaiah to the people with a message of judgment. "Also I heard the voice of the Lord, saying, Whom shall I send, and who will go for us? Then said I, Here am I; send me. And he said, Go, and tell this people, Hear ye indeed, but understand not; and see ye indeed, but perceive not. Make the heart of this people fat, and make their ears heavy, and shut their eyes; lest they see with their eyes, and hear with their ears, and understand with their hearts, and convert, and be healed. Then said I, Lord, how long? And he answered, Until the cities be wasted without inhabitant, and the houses without man, and the land be utterly desolate, And the Lord have removed men far away, and there be a great forsaking in the midst of the land" (Isaiah 6:8-12). As the evil days followed one another and as the sins of the people multiplied, Isaiah finally named the city of Babylon as the foreign land to which the people would be carried as slaves (Isaiah 39: 6, 7).

The prophet Micah was a contemporary of Isaiah. He, likewise, spoke of the coming judgment of the Almighty upon the sins of the nation. Then, like Isaiah before him, he also named Babylon as the land of the captivity. "Be in pain, and labour to bring forth, O daughter of Zion, like a woman in travail: for now shalt thou go forth out of the city, and thou shalt dwell in the field, and thou shalt go even to Babylon; there shalt thou be delivered; there the Lord shall redeem thee from the hand of thine enemies" (Micah 4:10).

The whole ministry of Jeremiah was a prophecy of doom ("the weeping prophet Jeremiah") and a heartbreaking plea to repent and to turn to the Lord. "When I would comfort myself against sorrow, my heart is faint in me. Behold the voice of the cry of the daughter of my people because of them that dwell in a far country: Is not the Lord in Zion? is not her king in her? Why have they provoked me to anger with their graven images, and with strange vanities? The harvest is past, the summer is ended, and we are not saved. For the hurt of the daughter of my people am I hurt; I am black; astonishment hath taken hold on me. Is there no balm in Gilead; is there no physician there? why then is not the health of the daughter of my people recovered? Oh that my head were waters, and mine eyes a fountain of tears, that I might weep day and night for the slain of the daughter of my people" (Jeremiah 8:18–9:1). "Then said the Lord unto me, Though Moses and Samuel stood before me, yet my mind could not be toward this people: cast them out of my sight, and let them go forth" (Jeremiah 15:1). "The sin of Judah is written with a pen of iron, and with the point of a diamond: it is graven upon the table of their heart, and upon the horns of your altars; Whilst their children remember their altars and their groves by the green trees upon the high hills" (Jeremiah 17:1, 2).

Did Judah heed these warnings from God? Does America today? Does the world tremble before The Almighty? No. Tragically, no. Sorrowfully, no. Disastrously, no. And judgment comes, inevitably comes.

4. Before the inexorable judgment of God upon the sins of Judah, the Lord gave the people opportunity after opportunity to get right in their personal, domestic, and na-

tional life. The account of His longsuffering is a story of amazing grace. Under good King Josiah God sent a great revival. It was a remarkable awakening, and it touched the nation from center to circumference. Not only this, but in the later days of Josiah the Assyrian Empire began to break up. What a golden future awaited a righteous, God-fearing, God-loving Judah!

But neither the outpouring of the blessings of God in the spiritual revival under Josiah, nor the defeat of the Assyrians had any permanent effects upon the wicked ways of Judah. Josiah was Judah's last good, God-fearing king. His successors, the kings of Judah, nullified Josiah's spiritual impact by their wickedness and idolatry. And when Assyria was destroyed, Babylon, "that bitter and hasty nation" (Habakkuk 1:6), took her place. When the prophet Habakkuk asked the Lord concerning the rise of the Chaldeans against Judah, the Lord replied, "I have ordained them for judgment and established them for correction" (Habakkuk 1:12). The rise of the Neo-Babylonian Empire was as meteoric as its demise. When its divine mission of chastening God's people was accomplished, it perished from the earth. But it was a bitter chastening rod in the hands of God. Nebuchadnezzar, one of the most powerful and autocratic of ancient rulers, adopted essentially the same policy of displacing whole populations as that inaugurated by the Assyrian kings. Thus, a nation's captivity insured the Empire against any further rebellion against the king. It forever removed the possibility of armed alliance against the throne. This policy also gave the victorious king slave labor to build his palaces and temples and cities, along with the skilled artisans and craftsmen for the execution of the elaborate program. Thus Judah fell into the hands of the Chaldeans under Nebuchadnezzar.

There were three deportations.

(1) The first was in 605 B.C. (Daniel 1:1-4), when Daniel and a few other of the seed royal were taken captive to glorify the court of the king at Babylon. Along with these

gifted young men were also carried some of the treasures of the Solomonic Temple.

(2) The second was in 598 B.C. (II Kings 24:10-17) when King Jehoiachin and all the royal family, the best of the land, the soldiers, and all the treasures of the Temple and of the king's house were carried away. In this group also was carried captive a young priest by the name of Ezekiel.

(3) The third and the final one was in 587 B.C. (II Kings 25:1-21) when the city and the Temple and the nation were destroyed and Judah ceased to be a sovereign state. The chief priests were put to death, the king was carried blinded to Babylon in chains where he soon died, and all the people (except the poorest of the land) were carried away captive to Babylon.

II. The Kings and the Prophets During the Days of the Captivity

The kings of Judah during the sorrowful days of the captivity were Jehoahaz, Jehoiakim, Jehoiachin, and Zedekiah. The prophets during those heartbreaking days were Jeremiah in Judah; his younger contemporary, Ezekiel, with the captives in Babylon; and Daniel, the statesman, in the court of Nebuchadnezzar.

The people of Judah did not realize the vast changes which were in store for them following the death of King Josiah, Judah's last good king. They doubtless expected Josiah's successors to continue the spiritual revival which came to such a glorious birth during his reign, and they also surely expected a continuation of his policy of political independence for Judah. Just the opposite prevailed in every aspect of the nation's life. The successors of Josiah were idolatrous and "did evil in the sight of the Lord," and brought the land to utter ruin. Reversing the policy of Josiah who sought to find freedom from the domination of Egypt, they formulated a new policy of depending upon Egypt for every hope of deliverance from foreign oppressors.

This was the express thing God told them not to do and the result was catastrophic. We shall follow the story under the succession of the kings and the warnings of the prophets.

1. *Jehoahaz,* II Kings 23:30-34

Upon the weakening of the Assyrian Empire (and its final dissolution) Pharaoh-Necho of Egypt saw an opportunity to seize Palestine and Syria, and eventually to control the civilized world. But first, the rising Babylonians must be defeated. Accordingly, he gathered a vast army and marched northward to aid the staggering Assyrians and to confront the advancing Chaldeans. King Josiah was no friend to the merciless Assyrians and when he saw Pharaoh going to their rescue, he placed his little Judean army in the way at Megiddo. The result was disastrous for Judah because in the battle that followed Josiah was slain. Upon Josiah's death "the people of the land" took one of his younger sons, Jehoahaz, and anointed him ruler over the nation. He reigned but three months, "doing evil in the sight of the Lord" (II Kings 23:32). He was removed by Pharaoh-Necho, who placed him in chains and took him to Egypt where he died. Necho then took another son of Josiah, Eliakim, and placed him on the throne, changing his name to Jehoiakim. Despite the fact that Necho had slain his father, good King Josiah, Jehoiakim was evidently pro-Egyptian, maybe the reason, "the people of the land" had passed him by to anoint his younger brother, Jehoahaz, to the throne. Jehoiakim was a passive tool in the hands of the Pharaoh for he gave the Egyptian enormous tribute of silver and gold, grievously taxing the people to do so (II Kings 23:35).

2. *Jehoiakim,* II Kings 23:34–24:6; Jeremiah 25, 36, 45, 46:1-12

When Pharaoh-Necho was defeated by Nebuchadnezzar at Carchemish and again at Hamath, the Babylonians followed the retreating Egyptians southward. This brought the Babylonian armies to Jerusalem and to the siege of the pro-Egyptian Judean king Jehoiakim, mentioned in Daniel

1:1. While Nebuchadnezzar was adding Syria and Palestine to his father's empire, word came that his father, Nabopolassar, had died. Nebuchadnezzar, accordingly, hastily returned to Babylon to be crowned king and to consolidate his victories at home. When he returned to the Chaldean capital from Judea, he took with him, in 605 B.C. (or soon thereafter), several of the finest youth of the land (among whom was Daniel) and some of the treasures of the Temple to place in the temple of his gods in Babylon. In all this he did not change the status of Jehoiakim. He left him king over the country.

But Jehoiakim, "who did evil in the sight of the Lord" (II Kings 23:37), after three years, rebelled against Nebuchadnezzar, relying not on God to help him but relying on Egypt. This hope of deliverance at the hands of the Egyptians was encouraged by false prophets (such as Hananiah, Jeremiah 28:1-17) and a pro-Egyptian party (Jeremiah 5:31, "the people love to have it so").

When Jeremiah the prophet raised a strong voice against the alliance with Egypt, Jehoiakim, the king, became his bitter enemy. The king imprisoned the prophet to keep him out of the Temple and away from the people (Jeremiah 36:5). Jeremiah then dictated to his amanuensis, Baruch, the message of the Lord God to Judah. King Jehoiakim had the scroll read to him leaf by leaf, and leaf by leaf "he cut it with his penknife, and cast it into the fire that was on the hearth, until all the roll was consumed in the fire that was on the hearth" (Jeremiah 36:23). Thus did Jehoiakim show his contempt for the Word of God. The answering flame of the wrath and fury of the Almighty Jehovah was fast and certain. The prophecy delivered by Jeremiah is recorded in Jeremiah 22:18, 19: "Therefore thus saith the Lord concerning Jehoiakim the son of Josiah king of Judah: They shall not lament for him, saying, Ah my brother! or, Ah sister! they shall not lament for him, saying Ah lord! or, Ah his glory! He shall be buried with the burial of an ass, drawn and cast forth beyond the gates of Jerusalem." No man can do dishonor to the Word of the

Lord and escape a falling, coming judgment. This applies to a nation, to a denomination, to an institution, to a prophet, to a church, to a preacher. The ringing words of I Samuel 2:30 forever stand: "Them that honor me I will honor, and they that despise me shall be lightly esteemed."

Upon the rebelling of Jehoiakim, the marching armies of Nebuchadnezzar reached Palestine again and Jerusalem was placed under siege. Before the city fell, Jehoiakim suddenly died (most likely he was assassinated) and his young eighteen-year-old son, Jehoiachin, was placed on the throne.

3. *Jehoiachin,* II Kings 24:6-16; Jeremiah 22:24-30

Jehoiachin, even though so young a man, was as evil as his father (II Kings 24:9). After his reign of a little more than three months, the city fell to the Babylonians, 598 B.C. The heartbreaking captivity that followed included the king, the queen's mother, the court, the soldiers, the craftsmen, the best of all the people of the land, the treasures of the Lord's house and of the king's palace, and a young priest by the name of Ezekiel. This carrying away into Babylon in 598 B.C. is commonly called "The Captivity" because of its magnitude and because of the king. The young Jehoiachin remained a prisoner in Babylon for thirty-seven years. Only upon the death of Nebuchadnezzar did his son and successor, Evil-Merodach, free him (II Kings 25:27, 28). This fact of the liberation of Jehoiachin, king of Judah, is written in Babylonian cuneiform records unearthed by modern day archaeologists.

The exiles always looked upon Jehoiachin as their legitimate king. Their dates were reckoned "from the exile of King Jehoiachin." This can be seen, for example, from the opening verses of the Book of Ezekiel: "Now it came to pass in the thirtieth year, in the fourth month, in the fifth day of the month, as I was among the captives by the river of Chebar, that the heavens were opened, and I saw visions of God. In the fifth day of the month, which was the fifth year of king Jehoiachin's captivity, The word of the Lord came expressly unto Ezekiel, the priest, the son of Buzi, in the land of the Chaldeans by the river Chebar; and the hand of the Lord was there upon him" (Ezekiel 1:1-3).

Jeremiah, the prophet in Judah, wrote to the exiles, saying that their stay would be long; in fact, seventy years, and for them to build homes and cultivate vineyards and fields. False prophets, such as Hananiah, said that Jehoiachin would be back in Judah as king within two years, but not Jeremiah. This true prophet of God, Jeremiah, said that the captivity would last nearly a century and the people (including Daniel) should prepare for the weary years (Jeremiah 28:1-17; 29:1-10).

4. *Zedekiah,* II Kings 24:17–25:11; Jeremiah 24, 27, 28, 32, 33, 34, 37, 38, 39, 51:59-64; 52.

When Nebuchadnezzar took Jehoiachin captive to Babylon, he placed upon the throne of Judah another of the ill-fated sons of Josiah, Mattaniah (an uncle of Jehoiachin) to whom he gave the name of Zedekiah. Zedekiah was as evil as his brother (II Kings 24:19) and his eleven-year reign in Jerusalem were years of fully ripened rebellion and corruption. Instead of turning to the Lord for help, he succumbed to the pro-Egyptian party and looked to the Pharaoh for deliverance from the heavy hand of Babylonia. When Zedekiah also (as the two kings before him had done) revolted against Nebuchadnezzar, the reaction of the Chaldean king was swift and terrible. This time he resolved to destroy the nation forever, sent by God to finish the work of judgment upon the sins of His people. By January, 588 B.C., Jerusalem was under siege (Jeremiah 52:4; II Kings 25:1).

The Word of the Lord repeatedly came to His prophet Jeremiah as God sought to warn the people. (Compare Jeremiah 24:1-10). During the early part of the siege, Jeremiah 34 was written. During the latter part of the siege Jeremiah 32, 33, 39:15-18 were written. And all during the siege the prophet suffered greatly because of these deliverances of God's message. He was accused of treason. The nobles of the city sought to have him put to death. He was cast into a vile prison and as the siege wore on, he was placed in a slimy pit (cistern) to die. However evil Zedekiah may have been, he had this one redeeming virtue: in his heart he seemed to desire to listen to Jeremiah and, whenever possible, he sought to spare his life. It was so in this case. When Jeremiah faced certain death in the miry pit, an Ethiopian eunuch named Ebed-melech pled with the king to grant him permission to lift him out of the horrible place. The king granted the request and the prophet was raised up out of the pit, even though it took thirty men to do it. So terrible and so disastrous was the raging famine, it took the effort of thirty men to do what otherwise one man could have done (Jeremiah 38:6-13).

After a siege of a year and a half, starvation and pestilence were increasingly rampant in the city. During the summer of 587 B.C. the end came. The walls were breached, and as the Chaldean armies poured into the city it was with the avowed purpose that the place would never be a source of rebellion again. The walls, the temple, the homes, the whole city were completely destroyed (II Chronicles 36:19). King Zedekiah attempted to escape toward Amman (II Kings 25:4, 5; Jeremiah 52:7, 8) but was captured near Jericho and brought to Nebuchadnezzar's headquarters at Riblah in central Syria on the Orontes River. There the sons of Zedekiah were slain before his eyes, then his own eyes were put out and he was taken in chains to Babylon, where he soon died (II Kings 25:6, 7).

Jeremiah was treated kindly by the victorious Babylonians (Jeremiah 39:11-14; 40:1–43:7). He was given the choice of remaining in the land or going with the captives to Babylon. He chose to stay with the poor who were left in the land and with their puppet governor, Gedaliah, whom Nebuchadnezzar had appointed over the people. But the people of Judah had not changed their evil ways. They assassinated Gedaliah and fled to Egypt, forcing Jeremiah to accompany them. In Egypt he died, after delivering God's messages recorded in Jeremiah 43:8–44:30. After this last and tragic rebellion, in 587 B.C., Judah ceased to exist as a sovereign state. Even the province of Judah was abolished after the murder of Gedaliah, and its territory was incorporated into the neighboring province of Samaria. Thus came to pass the Word of the Lord spoken by His holy prophets.

III. The Blessings That Came Out of the Captivity

Out of so grievous a sin on the part of the people of the Lord and out of so devastating a judgment on the part of the Sovereign of all the earth, could any good possibly come? Yes, yes indeed; for the sins of man cannot frustrate the ultimate purposes of God. God's heavy judgment upon Judah opened the way for the blessings of His sovereign grace. Five incomparable blessings came out of the sorrows of the captivity.

1. The nation was never again idolatrous. In the tragedies of the Babylonian exile the Jews were forever purged from their hankering after the cheap gods of wood, silver, stone and gold.

Can you imagine a Jew bowing down and worshiping before a graven image? There are three vast religious groups who refuse to make unto themselves idols of worship: the Jew, the Mohammedan, and the New Testament Christian. These three have that in common: they refuse to worship before a graven image, whether the image be named Jupiter or Joseph, Mercury or Mary. Idolatry is idolatry wherever it is found; namely, the use of images in worship. The Jew, the Mohammedan, and the New Testament Christian take to heart the solemnity of the second commandment (which the Roman church leaves out): "Thou shalt not make unto thee any graven image, or any likeness of anything that is in heaven above, or that is in the earth beneath, or that is in the water under the earth: Thou shalt not bow down thyself to them, nor serve them: for I the Lord thy God am a jealous God, visiting the iniquities of the fathers upon the children unto the third and fourth generation of them that hate me; and shewing mercy unto thousands of them that love me, and keep my commandments" (Exodus 20:4-6).

2. The institution of the synagogue was born in the Captivity. With the Temple destroyed, the gathering of the people came to be around the teaching priest and scribe, called the Rabbi. In his presence the people were taught to be obedient to the laws of Moses, to hear the words of the prophets, and to sing praises to Jehovah God. Our Christian churches today in their services are but extensions of the synagogue services born in the trials and tragedies of the Captivity. We are patterned after them in prayer, praises, preaching and Bible reading.

3. The canon of the Holy Scriptures was born in the Captivity. As the people wept in their despair, they sought the comfort and the promises of God's Word. This made the scrolls of the prophets of God doubly precious. Ezra and the men of God in the Great Synagogue gathered these scrolls together and the Old Testament Scriptures became the holy possessions of the people. "The grass withereth, the flower fadeth: but the word of our God shall stand forever" (Isaiah 40:8).

4. Out of the burning, purifying fires of the Exile came the faithful, godly remnant who, returning to Jerusalem and to Palestine, provided the seed which resulted in the coming of Christ. The Captivity gave to the people a new love for God, for the holy city of God, and for the precious worship of God, all in contrast to the heathen rituals they saw all around them. We cannot but sense the heart-beats and the tear-drops of the enslaved people as they said: "By the rivers of Babylon, there we sat down, yea, we wept, when we remembered Zion. We hanged our harps upon the willows in the midst thereof. For there they that carried us away captive required of us a song; and they that wasted us required of us mirth, saying, Sing us one of the songs of Zion. How shall we sing the Lord's song in a strange land? If I forget thee, O Jerusalem, let my right hand forget her cunning. If I do not remember thee, let my tongue cleave to the roof of my mouth; if I prefer not Jerusalem above my chief joy" (Psalm 137:1-6).

The Jews who returned from the Captivity carried with them the holy righteousness of a Joseph, a Mary, a James, a Peter, a John, a Paul.

5. In the dispersion of the people of Judah and of the other tribes of Israel came also the dispersion of the knowledge of the true God. The Jew finally covered the civilized world with his Sabbath, his ten commandments, and his Messianic hope. So absolutely and completely was the Jew dispersed over the nations of the globe that James, the pastor of the church at Jerusalem, could say in the first Jerusalem Conference: "For Moses of old time hath in every city them that preach him, being read in the synagogues every sabbath day" (Acts 15:21). Wherever the Christian evangelist and missionary went, there before him was the way prepared by the Jew with the Holy Scriptures in his hand and with the synagogue as a gathering place for their reading and expounding.

Thus the prophet-statesman Daniel stands in a heathen court to deliver God's message concerning "the times of the Gentiles," that great sweep of history beginning with the Captivity and extending to the days when Christ shall come again. Sometimes it is centuries before we are able to see God's sovereign purposes worked out. But work out, they will. The sweep of history leads to the victory of the kingdom which the God of heaven shall set up in those final, consummating days (Daniel 2:44). He will not fail. The saints shall inherit the earth. "And the kingdom and dominion, and the greatness of the kingdom under the whole heaven, shall be given to the people of the saints of the most High, whose kingdom is an everlasting kingdom, and all dominion shall serve and obey him" (Daniel 7:27). "Fear not, little flock; for it is your Father's good pleasure to give you the kingdom" (Luke 12:32).

Chapter IX

THE FORMATIVE YEARS OF DANIEL'S LIFE

> In the third year of the reign of Jehoiakim king of Judah came Nebuchadnezzar king of Babylon unto Jerusalem, and besieged it. And the Lord gave Jehoiakim king of Judah into his hands, with part of the vessels of the house of God: which he carried into the land of Shinar to the house of his god; and he brought the vessels into the treasurer house of his god. And the king spake unto Ashpenaz the master of his eunuchs, that he should bring certain of the children of Israel, and of the king's seed, and of the princes; Children in whom was no blemish, but well favoured, and skilful in all wisdom, and cunning in knowledge, and understanding science, and such as had ability in them to stand in the king's palace, in whom they might teach the learning and the tongue of the Chaldeans. . . . Now among these were of the children of Judah, Daniel, Hananiah, Mishael, and Azariah. . . . But Daniel purposed in his heart that he would not defile himself with the portion of the king's meat, nor with the wine which he drank.
>
> Daniel 1:1-4, 6, 8a

As we prepare to enter into the life of the prophet Daniel we have many opportunities to acquaint ourselves with those influences that made him the glorious figure he came to be in God's prophetic world. Both in the Holy Scriptures and from profane secular sources we have full recourse to an intimate description of the days in which Daniel's life and lot were cast. The youth of Daniel is particularly interesting to us now because his after years reflected the godly training and the tremendous decisions he made during the time he lived in Judaea and Jerusalem. We shall, therefore, turn to the story of God's chosen people before the days of the Babylonian captivity to acquaint ourselves with the early story that so deeply influenced the life of God's beloved exile.

I. His Birth

1. Daniel was born about 625 B.C. in one of those unusual chronological coincidences that sometimes occur in history. The year 625 B.C. is also the birth date of the Neo-Babylonian Empire. Ashurbanipal, the last mighty king of Assyria, died in 625 B.C. His son, Ashuruballit, was weak and incapable. The year, therefore, that this weak son of Ashurbanipal ascended the Assyrian throne, his viceroy in the Province of Babylon, Nabopolassar, the father of Nebuchadnezzar, rebelled and took all of Babylonia out of the Assyrian Empire. Incidentally, this is the reason for the statement found in Daniel 1:21. "And Daniel continued even unto the first year of king Cyrus" (Daniel 1:21). Yet Daniel 10:1 says that the prophet saw a vision in the third year of Cyrus king of Persia. What could it mean, therefore, when Daniel 1:21 avows that the prophet continued even unto the first year of King Cyrus? The answer is found in the intent of the verse in Daniel 1:1; namely, that the life of Daniel spanned the entire Babylonian captivity of seventy years, yea, and included the entire length of the whole Babylonian Empire. Daniel was born in 625 B.C., the birth date of the Babylonian Empire, and he continued throughout the course of Nebuchadnezzar's reign and throughout the course of his successors, even until the day that the Babylonian Empire fell under the conquest of Cyrus, king of Persia.

2. Many of the destiny-determining events of all history occurred during Daniel's lifetime, several of them during his boyhood. Of these, one of the greatest was the fall of Nineveh in 612 B.C., a fact which changed the course of his-

tory, made Babylon the new master of Western Asia and Nabopolassar, with his son Nebuchadnezzar, the most powerful ruler in the civilized world. In 612 B.C. Nabopolassar with his Chaldean army, along with Cyaxares, king of the Medes, with his Median army destroyed Nineveh forever. This significant and mighty event had deep and everlasting repercussion in the life of the nation of Judah and in the life of the young man Daniel.

3. Daniel was a child of the royal house, of kingly nobility, reared in close touch with the highest personages of the nation. The profound effect of these Jewish national and political leaders upon his life is seen throughout the after years. First among these men of high estate stood the great and good King Josiah. Josiah had been ruler over the nation about fifteen years when Daniel was born. Perhaps next to Daniel himself, Josiah was dearer to the heart of God and to the hearts of the people than any other king (II Chronicles 34:2, 3). It was King Josiah who led the nation into one of the greatest revivals of all history.

II. The Great Revival in Daniel's Boyhood

Daniel was old enough to catch the thrill and the inspiration of the blessed outpouring of God's mercy and grace during the reign of King Josiah. Josiah, who ruled for thirty-one years, came to the throne at eight years of age (II Chronicles 34:1). At fifteen or sixteen years of age he gave his heart to God (II Chronicles 34:3). We would say that at that age he was wondrously and marvelously converted. In the commitment of his life to the Lord, Josiah did some glorious things for Jehovah and was used of the Lord to bring to the people an incomparable blessing.

1. He sought to undo the fifty-seven shameless years of his grandfather and his father, both of whom brought the nation to the very brink of idolatrous destruction. His grandfather, Manasseh, who reigned fifty-five years, led Judah down to her deepest degradation. When he was carried by Assyria in chains to provincial Babylon, he repented of his

sins, but when he was returned to his throne he was unable to undo the evil he had already wrought. Josiah was six years old when his grandfather Manasseh died. Josiah's father, King Amon, was as wicked as any monarch who reigned in Judah. He occupied the throne but two years, after which he was slain by a conspiracy of slaves in his own house. This brought to the kingdom the boy Josiah, eight years of age. But when he was converted in the eighth year of his reign, he sought, with all the help that God could give him, to bring the nation back to the Lord. He destroyed idolatry in Judah and reestablished the moral worship of Jehovah.

2. Josiah was mightily helped in his revival of God's true religion by the prophets whom the Lord raised up during those days. It was in the thirteenth year of the reign of Josiah that God commissioned Jeremiah to preach (Jeremiah 1:2). For the first eighteen years of the prophet's ministry, he preached under the aegis of Josiah. As Jeremiah undertook the task of internal and spiritual reform, Josiah assumed the responsibility of external, political renewal. Not only did God send Jeremiah in those days of tremendous revival, but also Zephaniah began to preach, and in the latter years of Josiah's reign, Nahum appeared with God's message. These prophets mightily strengthened the hand of the king in his work for the Lord.

3. God placed it in the heart of King Josiah to repair the temple erected by Solomon (II Kings 22:3-7; II Chronicles 34:8-13). While the king, in the eighteenth year of his reign, began to repair the house of the Lord, a marvelous thing came to pass. The Book of Law was found in the Temple (II Kings 22:8-11; II Chronicles 34:14-19). What an unusual and an amazing thing! That the Bible could be lost in the church, in the house of God! But when we look in our modern pulpits the tragedy of a lost Bible in God's house is repeated a thousand times a thousand times. In so many pulpits of the modern world the Bible is looked upon as a piece of antique literature with no more authority

than any other document that has survived the ravages of time. In so many sermons the Bible is never read, is never referred to, and in many instances the name of Jesus is never called. The deep darkness that overwhelmed the kingdom of Judah in the days of Manasseh and Amon has overspread so much of our modern Christian world. No greater tragedy could overtake us.

How could it have been that the Bible had been lost to the people and was only discovered when the Temple was under repair? It could be that the wicked king, Manasseh, and his equally wicked son, Amon, had destroyed the Scriptures, taking pains to wipe out even the written Word of God. In any event, the Book of the Law had ceased to be known in the land, and when it was discovered, the finding was a marvelous intervention of God's grace.

The Book, apparently, was found by the construction workers in the Temple. The discovery is closely connected with the activity of the stone masons and the carpenters. We can remember in after years that Nabonidus, the father of Belshazzar, was an antiquarian and an archeologist more than he was a politician and a commander-in-chief of the army. Nabonidus left his eldest son, Belshazzar, in charge of the throne in Babylon while he delighted himself with digging into the foundations of buildings ancient even in his day to recover documents deposited there centuries before. In like manner, possibly the copy of the Pentateuch had been placed in the cornerstone of the Temple when it was erected by Solomon around 966 B.C. It is possible that the masonry had so deteriorated through the passing centuries that the cornerstone had to be replaced or reset, and this brought its contents to light. From time immemorial builders have placed documents of lasting interest in public buildings as they have dedicated the cornerstone in its erection.

In any event, this Book of God was found by the workmen and placed in the hands of Hilkiah, the high priest, who, in turn, delivered it to Shaphan, the scribe, who, in turn, read it to King Josiah. When the king heard the word of the Book of God, he rent his garments in repentance and in contrition over the neglect of God's Word on the part of the nation. The king then called a great convocation of the leaders of the people to the Temple where the Book of God was read to them (II Kings 23:2). This was national revival in itself. God ever blesses His Word to the glory and the exaltation of a people who will read it and heed it in love and godly devotion.

4. Out of this reading of God's Word and out of the revival led by King Josiah came one of the greatest passovers ever observed in the history of Judah (II Kings 23:21-23; II Chronicles 35:1-19). Josiah's godly efforts were crowned with this most glorious of passovers. It was observed in a manner unprecedented in Judah's history. It reflected the marvelous revival that God gave to the people during those epochal years.

III. Daniel's Spiritual Strength

Out of this revival came the spiritual strength that carried Daniel through the following years of tragedy and captivity.

1. At the very height of the revival and during the zenith of Josiah's leadership, the great and good king was slain (II Kings 23:29, 30; II Chronicles 35:20-25). When Daniel was about sixteen years old, this tragedy, unparalleled in the history of Judah, befell the nation. Josiah was killed by the armies of Pharaoh-Necho at Megiddo when he tried to stop the northern march of Necho through the valley of Jezreel.

(a) Why did Josiah interfere with the northward thrust of Pharaoh-Necho? The Authorized version and the American Revised version read in II Kings 23:29 that Necho was proceeding "against the king of Assyria." Reading this version, we are profoundly perplexed as to why Josiah sought to stop Necho, when the Pharaoh was on his way to fight the ancient enemy of the Hebrews; namely, the Assyrians. The cruel and merciless Assyrians had oppressed Israel for centuries. In 722 B.C. Sargon destroyed Samaria and carried away the northern ten tribes into captivity. In 701 B.C. Sennacherib laid seige to Jerusalem and, according to his record of the campaign, he carried about two hundred fifty thousand of the people of Judah as slaves into his own country. What could it mean, therefore, when the Authorized version says that Necho was marching against the king of Assyria and that King Josiah sought to stop him?

Archaeology has brought to light the special meaning of the Hebrew proposition translated "against." We now know that Necho did not advance against the Assyrians at all but went to their aid. To stop that assistance, Josiah placed his little army in the way to prevent Necho reaching the hard-pressed Assyrians. It was because Josiah did not want to see the Assyrians helped that he risked his life and that of his army to prevent the Egyptians from reaching the Assyrians.

But even with good cause, why did Josiah think he could stop Necho? This is apparently the one and only misstep in the life of this good and great king; namely, this misguided and foolish interference with Egypt's attempt to gain supremacy over Babylon through friendship with the waning, decaying power of Assyria. We know that later Necho was defeated at the battle of Carchemish in 605 B.C. and the power of Egypt was forever broken. From that day until this she has never been the head of a great empire, nor, according to the Word of God, will she ever be. In the sovereignty of the Almighty there was no need whatsoever for Josiah's interference. God took care of Egypt as God judges all nations of the world. Why then did Josiah interfere? Apparently, God's blessing upon him caused him to engage in this presumptuous, political act. Because God had so marvelously crowned his efforts with every heavenly favor in days past, he presumed that God would no less bless him in his political ambitions and in his extended acts of state.

This reminds us that it is not in our defeat and in our humility that we are most likely to presume upon God, but rather, in our successes come our greatest temptations to presumption. In defeat we are bowed down. We are humbled. We cast ourselves upon the mercies of the Lord. In success we are so often proud and lifted up, and it is pride that goeth before a fall. This, apparently, is what happened to good King Josiah. God had so wondrously blessed him in other days that he was led into this presumptuous interference with the armies of Egypt, thinking that God would give him victory in this decision. In any event, Josiah was slain and that brought to a conclusion the great revival in Judah.

(b) The lamentation over Josiah was deep and bitter. II Chronicles 35:25 reads: "And Jeremiah lamented for Josiah: and all the singing men and the singing women spake of Josiah in their lamentations to this day, and made them an ordinance in Israel: and, behold, they are written in the lamentations." Years and years later the prophet Zechariah wrote: "And I will pour upon the house of David, and upon the inhabitants of Jerusalem, the spirit of grace and of supplications: and they shall look upon me whom they have pierced, and they shall mourn for him, as one mourneth for his only son, and shall be in bitterness for him, as one that is in bitterness for his firstborn. In that day shall there be a great mourning in Jerusalem, as the mourning of Hadad-rimmon in the valley of Megiddon. And the land shall mourn, every family apart; the family of the house of David apart, and their wives apart; the family of the house of Nathan apart, and their wives apart; The family of the house of Levi apart, and their wives apart; the family of Shimei apart; and their wives apart; all the families that remain, every family apart, and their wives apart" (Zechariah 12: 10-14). What is this Hadad-rimmon in the valley of Megiddon? Hadad-rimmon is the place where Josiah lay mortally wounded and at a later date, after his death, all Judah gathered there for a lamentation that was never forgotten. The death of King Josiah was one of the greatest tragedies that ever happened in the life of God's people.

2. The revival under Josiah had no effect upon his own family. When Josiah died, his sons and successors took not

up the mantle of their godly father, but they took up the mantle, of their godless grandfather, Amon, and their even more godless great grandfather, Manasseh. The sons of Josiah sought to undo as rapidly as possible all that their devoted father had done. The wicked Jehoahaz (called Shallum in Jeremiah 22:11, 12) was carried captive down to Egypt, where he died. The wicked Jehoiakim, another son of Josiah, was buried with the burial of an ass, according to the Word of the Lord delivered by Jeremiah. You remember it was Jehoiakim who cut up the prophecies of Jeremiah with his penknife and burned them on the grate in the winter fire. The wicked Zedekiah, another son of Josiah, saw his own son slain before his very eyes, his own eyes put out with rods of heated iron, and then was carried in fetters to Babylon where he died. The wicked Jehoiachin, the son and successor Jehoiakim, and the grandson of King Josiah, languished as a captive in Babylon for thirty-seven years. The real revival had no effect and no repercussion, whatsoever, in the lives of Josiah's own family and, seemingly, no effect in the life of the nation. The people quickly and immediately returned to their vile, idolatrous practices.

3. But the revival had a glorious and marvelous repercussion in the life of the youthful Daniel.

(a) His family lived in a home in which the law of God was observed and honored. The impressionable heart of the lad was affected profoundly and indelibly. From boyhood he knew no other thing than to love and to obey the Word of God.

(b) Following Josiah's death and the plunging of the nation into rampart idolatry, he formed attitudes of faithfulness to God that never changed. The sudden and extreme contrast now introduced into his political and moral surroundings made the decision to serve God the more meaningful in his life. As the kingdom of Judah reeled dizzily in wanton idolatry and wickedness, Daniel girded himself to withstand rather than to drift with the current of his time. The great revival may have been lost upon the wicked

Jehoahaz and Jehoiakim and Zedekiah and Jehoiachin, but the revival found a glorious response in the hearts of Daniel and Hananiah and Mishael and Azariah.

(c) When the tragedy of Daniel's captivity came to pass, as he was true to God at home in Judah he was true to God away from home in Babylon. As he was in Jerusalem so he was in Babylon. He was *in* Babylon but not *of* it. He was as out and out for God in Babylon as he was in Jerusalem. As a captive he was under the iron fist of a heathen king but as a child of God he was under the gracious hand of the Lord. The revival lived in Daniel throughout the years of his life. It never faded, or waned, or died.

4. As I think of the effect of the revival in the life of Daniel, my soul is flooded with a thousand memories of the effect of revival in my own life. I was saved in a revival meeting in a little white crackerbox of a church house, in a small town. I can remember as though it were yesterday the men and the women who refused the overtures of God's grace. But I responded. I went down the aisle and gave my hand to the preacher and my heart to the Lord. They refused as did the wicked sons of Josiah, but God had mercy upon me and I was saved.

I remember the revival when I responded to God's call to preach. During those days of the outpouring of the Holy Spirit there were many who refused God's overtures of grace, but I responded and answered with my life. In my first revival meetings and through the meetings that I have conducted through the years, there have been strong men who have refused to respond to God's love and grace, but God has always given us some. The Word of the Lord may fall upon deaf ears and upon stony hearts, but it will also fall upon good ground and upon hungry hearts and in that the Lord has never failed to give us a harvest. We are never to be discouraged. There will never come a time in this age and dispensation when all will be saved; but, likewise, there will never be a time when all refuse. In the sovereign grace and in the elective purpose of the Almighty, His Word will never return unto Him void. It will prosper in that purpose to which God has sent it. We are, therefore, to be faithful in the delivery of God's message, knowing that the Holy Spirit will work with us in triumph and in soul-saving success. If not all are saved, some will be; and these are trophies of grace that we can lay at the feet of our Saviour.

Chapter X

DANIEL AND REVELATION

> . . . and Daniel had understanding in all visions and dreams . . .
>
> Daniel 1:17b

The Book of Daniel had a tremendous influence upon the life and literature of the Jewish people during the centuries following its publication. This influence extended through the inter-Testamental period down to the times and to the writers of the New Testament. In fact, the vast influence of the prophecy helped to shape and color the Christian community for the years following the foundation and building of the church.

1. The Book of Daniel was loved, studied, known, and quoted by our Saviour. We have but to look at these following comparisons between the words and thoughts of our Lord and the language and visions of the Book of Daniel to see how much of Daniel was in the thought and words of our Lord. Matthew 24:15 equals Daniel 9:27; 11:31; 12:11. Matthew 24:21 equals Daniel 12:1. Matthew 24:30 equals Daniel 7:13. Matthew 26:64 equals Daniel 7:13. John 5: 28, 29 equal Daniel 12:2. Matthew 14:43 equals Daniel 12: 3. All of these passages but emphasize the close study of the Book by our Lord Jesus Christ.

2. The Book of Daniel was no less made a part of the study and spiritual searching of Paul, Peter and the author of The Hebrews. Paul, in I Corinthians 6:2, refers to Daniel 7:22, where the avowal is made that the saints will judge

the world. Paul, in II Thessalonians 2:3, describes the ultimate man of sin in the same imagery that Daniel presents the boasting of the little horn in Daniel 7:8. Paul fills out the outline that Daniel previously had sketched. Paul refers to the Book of Daniel in the last chapter of his last letter, II Timothy 4:17. The author of Hebrews refers to the prophet Daniel in 11:33 and to the three Hebrew children in Hebrews 11:34. Simon Peter makes a reference in I Peter 1:10 to Daniel 9:3; 12:8. These passages but reflect the close study of this Old Testament prophetic Book on the part of the authors of the New Testament.

3. But however much the Book of Daniel may have been in the hands of the Lord Jesus and of the Apostles, the volume was especially loved, studied, and quoted by the beloved disciple, John. From the heavenly point of view, the Revelation, the last book in the Bible, was a gift of God to us through Jesus Christ. The same author of the visions given to Daniel is the same author of the visions given to John. But from the earthly point of view there is so much of Daniel to be seen in the Revelation. It will be most profitable, therefore, to compare the two authors and their two books.

I. A Comparison of the Two Authors

1. Both Daniel and John were highly favored of heaven. Both men were greatly beloved by men and by angels. Daniel thrice is called "the man greatly beloved" (Daniel 9:23; 10:11, 19). John five times is called "the disciple whom Jesus loved" (John 13:23; 19:26; 20:2; 21:7, 20). Both men were chosen of heaven for the privilege of seeing the vision of the whole course of time from 605 B.C. on down to the second coming of Christ and the consummation of the age. No other men in all the history of humanity were ever so signally and so unusually favored.

2. Both men wrote apocalyptically. In this they were both unusual among the authors of the Bible. (Zechariah 1-6 and Ezekiel 37 are apocaplyptic; beside these passages

and the Books of Daniel and Revelation there is little of the apocalyptic in the Bible.) Daniel occupies the same office among Old Testament writers as John the Seer does among New Testament writers. The Book of Daniel is the apocalypse of the Old Testament (the first of the centuries of apocalyptic literature that followed). The Book of the Revelation is the apocalypse of the New Testament. The Old Testament book cannot be understood without the New Testament book, nor can the New Testament book be understood without the Old Testament book. They mutually explain, substantiate, and corroborate each other.

Apocalyptic writing, by the way, is one of the most unique developments in the literature of the race. It is a literary vehicle by which the message is carried in signs, symbols, and visions. In the Bible it is characterized by the presence of a divine interpreter and the subject matter here and elsewhere pertains to the end-time. For the most part, apocalyptic writing was produced at a time when God's people were under terrific persecution and the purpose of the vision was to give encouragement, hope, and promised victory for God's distressed people.

3. Both men saw their visions in exile. Daniel was a captive in the court of the kings of Babylon and Medo-Persia. John was an exile from his beloved people at Ephesus and was sentenced to exposure on the lonely, rocky island of Patmos. But there is no place where God is not in comfort and in holy presence attending the lives and lot of his chosen servants. God was with Daniel in Babylon as he had been with him in Jerusalem. The Lord Jesus Christ was no less with John on Patmos than He was with him in his beloved pastorate at Ephesus. To both men in exile God revealed Himself in unusual grace and power.

II. A Comparison of the Two Books

No more profitable study could be made by a student of God's Holy Word than to compare the twelve chapters of the Book of Daniel with the twenty-two chapters of the

Book of the Revelation. If one would know at all of God's outline for the future, the study of these two books and a comparison of their visions of the future are immediately and eternally profitable.

1. Both writings are books of prophecy. Revelation is a prophecy. The book is five times so described (Revelation 1:3; 22:7, 10, 18, 19). When I read that the Book of Revelation is a prophecy, I am consequently to remember that the things I read have a meaning beyond themselves. For example, the messages of our Lord in the second and third chapters of the Book of the Revelation to the Seven Churches of Asia have a profound significance in themselves. But there is a meaning in the messages that reaches beyond those particular local churches in Asia. The Revelation is a book of prophecy and I am to see in the message an unfolding of God through Christian history beyond that particular day and time in which the apocalypse was written. There were many more churches in Asia than just those seven named in chapters two and three. For example, right across the Lycus River from Laodicea was located the city of Hierapolis, where Papias, the disciple of John, was pastor. But Hierapolis is not referred to; nor are any other of the many churches of the Roman Province of Asia. These seven churches are representative churches, and they have a prophetic purpose in the addresses of our Lord.

We find a like instance of this deeply significant meaning beyond what actually is named and described in the Gospel of John. John, in his gospel, never uses the word "miracle," but he unvaryingly uses the word "sign" (Greek "Semeion"). The things Jesus did were not so much miracles as they were signs pointing to profound spiritual reality. The miracle (John calls it a sign) of the water turned into wine is a picture of the filling up of the old foot tubs and washing pots and legal requirements of the old law and then finding rejoicing and thanksgiving for the new faith and the new religion in the love and mercy of Jesus Christ. The old is passing away, having been fulfilled, and the new is being offered through the preaching of the gospel of the

Son of God. It is thus throughout John's gospel. The opening of the eyes of the blind man is a picture of Jesus, the light of the world. The raising of Lazarus from the dead is a marvelous illustration of our Lord as our resurrection and our life.

Thus and so, we are to remember in our study of the Book of Daniel that the volume is primarily and first of all a prophecy. In our study of the book we are to remember that beyond the things we read are the all significant spiritual connotations that lie beyond the actual verse itself. Daniel was a statesman-prophet, but of the two tremendous offices that he held, Jesus emphasized the latter. In Matthew 24:14, He refers to Daniel as a prophet. The broad meaning of the word "prophet" refers to a man who speaks for God, who delivers God's message. The narrower use of the word "prophet" refers to a man who foretells the future. In this narrower sense Jesus uses the word "prophet" to refer to Daniel. In our Lord's own judgment he is a man who unfolded the future.

In the Book of Daniel, therefore, we are to see in every part of it a prophetic meaning. The book is divided into two divisions. Chapters 1 through 6 are history. Chapters 7 through 12 are prophecy. Yet all the chapters are prophetic. Chapter 1 is the story of the captivity of the four Hebrew children. But the chapter is also a picture of the diaspora, the scattering of God's people throughout the earth. Chapter 2 contains the story of the dream of King Nebuchadnezzar. But it is also a summation of the entire course of the times of the Gentiles. Chapter 3 recounts the story of the three Hebrew children in the fiery furnace. But it is also a picture of Israel, God's people, in the fiery furnace of the tribulation.

Chapter 4 is the story of Nebuchadnezzar's dream of the giant tree cut down which found new life and new birth in the mercy of God. This is a picture of the Gentile nations of the earth which are cut down in the awful days of judgment, but who are raised up to glorify God. It tells us of the forgiveness and intervention of our Saviour from heaven.

The chapter is a picture of the millennial conversion of the nations of the earth. Let us read again Daniel 4:1-3: "Nebuchadnezzar the king, unto all people, nations, and languages, that dwell in all the earth; Peace be multiplied unto you. I thought it good to shew the signs and wonders that the high God hath wrought toward me. How great are his signs! and how mighty are his wonders! his kingdom is an everlasting kingdom, and his dominion is from generation to generation." These are not the words of an Old Testament saint. They are the words of a heathen king. They are prophetic of the words that will one day be spoken by the rulers and nations of the earth.

Chapter 5 recounts the story of the handwriting on the wall. This is a prophetic picture of the judgment of God on the Gentile governments of the earth. Chapter 6 is the unusual story of the preservation of Daniel in the lions' den. It is, also, a prophetic picture of the preservation of Israel, God's people, who are buried in the den of Gentile domination. The story is also an encouragement for all of the Lord's people who are called upon to suffer for His name's sake (II Timothy 4:17). Withal, we are to remember that the whole book, all the chapters, all the verses, all the dreams and visions, all the stories are prophetic. The Book of Daniel, like the Book of the Revelation, is a book of prophecy.

2. Both the Book of Daniel and the Book of the Revelation deal with the events of this age in which we live and with the events of the end of time. So much that was sealed in Daniel is unsealed, revealed, opened, in the Revelation. For example, let us read Daniel 12:8, 9: "And I heard, but I understood not: then said I, O my Lord, what shall be the end of these things? And he said, Go thy way, Daniel: for the words are closed up and sealed till the time of the end." Having read these verses in Daniel, let us turn to the fifth chapter of the Book of the Revelation and read the first five verses. What was hidden from the eyes of Daniel, what was sealed in his book of prophecy, is open to view in the Revelation.

This tremendously significant fact accounts for the differing emphases in the two books. Daniel recounts the course of Gentile history to the consummation of the age, but the consummation, itself, was largely hidden from his eyes. The details of the end time were sealed as far as Daniel was concerned. The Revelation, on the other hand, is the unsealing and the revealing of the end time. The first part of the Book of the Revelation follows the history of the church to the time of the rapture, the translation of the church to heaven. This period of the history of the church was absolutely and completely unknown to Daniel, as to all of the other Old Testament prophets. This age of grace and of the calling out of the body of Christ was a mystery, a secret kept in the heart of God until it was revealed to the Apostles. This is fully explained by the Apostle Paul in the third chapter of Ephesians. This history of the church, therefore, that was sealed to the eyes of the prophet Daniel is revealed to John and is made known in the Revelation. In the Book of Daniel the end time is so briefly referred to, such as in the ninth chapter of Daniel, in his reference to the seventieth week of the tribulation. On the other hand, the Apostle John devotes Chapters 4 through 19 to a detailed outline of that seventieth week, called "the tribulation." What was barely mentioned and scantily sketched in Daniel is fully and boldly revealed in the Revelation.

There is one thing, however, that both books present in most graphic and descriptive outline. One of the chief actors in the Book of Daniel is the man of sin, the final Anti-Christ, the one who exalts himself above God. This is also to be found in the Revelation. One of the chief actors of the final tribulation is this man of sin, this final Anti-Christ, this beast that arises out of the sea. Paul, himself, in the second chapter of II Thessalonians spoke so clearly and so definitely of this final world dictator.

Both Daniel and the Revelation describe in beautiful and marvelous language the glorious coming of our Lord Jesus Christ. Daniel speaks of it in these words:

> I saw in the night visions, and, behold, one like the Son of man came with the clouds of heaven, and came to

> the Ancient of days, and they brought him near before him.
>
> And there was given him dominion, and glory, and a kingdom, that all people, nations, and languages, should serve him: his dominion is an everlasting dominion, which shall not pass away, and his kingdom that which shall not be destroyed (Daniel 7:13, 14).

John describes that marvelous and heavenly intervention in these words:

> And I saw heaven opened, and behold a white horse; and he that sat upon him was called Faithful and True, and in righteousness he doth judge and make war.
>
> His eyes were as a flame of fire, and on his head were many crowns: and he had a name written, that no man knew, but he himself.
>
> And he was clothed with a vesture dipped in blood: and his name is called The Word of God.
>
> And the armies which were in heaven followed him upon white horses, clothed in fine linen, white and clean.
>
> And out of his mouth goeth a sharp sword, that with it he should smite the nations: and he shall rule them with a rod of iron: and he treadeth the winepress of the fierceness and wrath of Almighty God.
>
> And he hath on his vesture and on his thigh a name written, KING OF KINGS, AND LORD OF LORDS (Revelation 19:11-16).

To both Daniel and John, the final triumph of the Kingdom of God is sure and certain. It is God's sovereign will that the saints shall inherit the earth and we shall achieve this incomparable victory through Christ Jesus our Lord.

3. So much of the thoughts and words of the Book of Daniel are in the Book of the Revelation. We are not surprised at this because the great God in heaven revealed to both authors the vast program of history that lay ahead. However, from the earthly point of view, it can easily be seen that the author of the Book of the Revelation knew and studied closely the Book of Daniel.

(1) In the historical section of Daniel (Chapters 1-6)

there are many passages that are re-echoed in the Revelation. For example, "The things that shall come to pass hereafter" of Revelation 1:19; 4:1 is an echo of Daniel 2:29, 45. The ten days trial of Revelation 2:10 is an echo of Daniel 1:12, 15. The gods of silver and gold which see not and hear not of Revelation 9:20 is an echo of Daniel 5:23. The forty-two months, the one thousand two hundred sixty days, the time, times and half a time, of Revelation 11:2, 3; 12:14 is an echo of Daniel 7:25; 12:11; 12:7. The vision of the compelling of all men to worship the image in Revelation 13:15 is an echo of Daniel 3:6. The great Babylon, referred to in Revelation 18:2, is an echo of Daniel 4:30. The sweeping away of the fragments of world power so that no place was found for them, in Revelation 20:11 is an echo of Daniel 2:35. It is thus throughout the whole Book of the Revelation. The words and thoughts and language of the historical section of Daniel can be seen so effectively and so emphatically in the Revelation.

(2) There are many passages in the prophetic section of Daniel (Chapters 7 through 12) that are clearly explained in the Revelation. It is in this area that the Revelation so wondrously complements the prophecy of Daniel.

(a) Daniel 7:13, 14 presents one of the sublimest visions ever revealed to man. But who is this wondrous person who comes before the Ancient of Days? Revelation 1:7, and the verses that follow, describe that exalted person precisely and exactly. He is none other than the crucified Lord Jesus who is coming again in infinite glory and power. This was the avowal that Jesus made before the Jewish high priest as His words are recorded in Matthew 26:64. Jesus herein says that His death is to lead the way to the glory with which He would appear in His second advent. In Revelation 14:14 the exact language of Daniel 7:13 is used to describe the person of that ultimate and final judge who is coming to reap the harvest of the ultimate and final judge who is coming to reap the harvest of the earth. He is one likened to the Son of Man coming on a white cloud. In Revelation

1:13-15 we read the glorious description of the incomparable and immortalized Lord Jesus. So much of this description is taken from the prophecy of Daniel.

Revelation 1:14, 15; 2:18 equals Daniel 10:5, 6. Revelation 1:17 equals Daniel 10:8-11. Revelation 1:17 equals Daniel 10:12. Revelation 10:5, 6 equals Daniel 12:7. Revelation 20:15 equals Daniel 12:1. John 5:27 also refers to this great judgment.

The Revelation fully and clearly depicts the glorious Person who is presented in the prophecy of Daniel.

(b) As we read Daniel 7:7, 19, 20, and follow it with the reading of Revelation 13 and 17, there is no doubt as to the identity of this fourth kingdom described by the Hebrew prophet. Revelation 13:1, 2 describes the beast that rose out of the sea. In the Revelation the prophet does not look upon four successive wild beasts, as in Daniel 7:2-7, but only one. This indicates that three have already risen and passed and the one remaining is the fourth and last kingdom. Daniel described this beast as a nondescript; that is, not like any particular animal. John described it as being an amalgamation of the three wild beasts which preceded it in the Book of Daniel: that is, it had the likeness of a leopard, which is Daniel's third kingdom; the likeness of a bear, which is Daniel's second kingdom; and the likeness of a lion, which is Daniel's first kingdom. The fourth and final kingdom included all the rest in its gigantic world sway. As in Daniel, so in the Revelation, the power of the beast is derived from Satan (Revelation 13:2). These are but typical instances of the filling in of detail that the Revelation adds to the outline of history revealed to the prophet Daniel.

III. A Comparison of the Two Theologies

A lifetime could be spent in studying and in presenting the great apocalyptic, eschatological theology of Daniel and the Revelation. Literally libraries have been written concerning this study. We have but a moment here to write of the great basic outline of history in which the two authors completely and absolutely agree. Daniel 2:44 and 7:9-14 clearly reveal that there is a coming kingdom of the Lord God that shall be established apocalyptically in this earth. The great stone, in Daniel 2:34, smites the image on the feet; that is, during the last eras of human history. Daniel 2:35 plainly states that the fragments of world empire are completely swept away. Instead of these broken and decimated kingdoms, God establishes an empire that includes all humanity, all the earth, and that endures throughout all eternity.

This is the triumphant vision of Revelation 19:11 following, and Revelation 20:1 following. In Revelation 19:11 the Lord Jesus Christ intervenes in human history at the Battle of Armageddon. The following verses and chapters describe the millennial reign of our Lord after the binding of Satan and the ultimate new heaven and new earth wherein God's people shall reign with their Lord forever and ever.

Whether we read of the kingdom in Daniel, or whether we read of the kingdom in the Revelation, both prophecies are the same. The history of the Gentile nations of the earth continues in broken fragments and under the domination of evil until the whole corpus is swept away by the coming of the King of Kings and by the establishment of a heavenly reign through Christ our Lord.

Will such a day ever come? Yes, and most certainly. The third chapter of II Peter was written for us, lest we be discouraged in the long years and centuries of waiting. By God's time clock a thousand years is but a day. By God's time clock our Saviour has been ascended into heaven after His resurrection from the dead only two days. It may be that in the third day He will come again. In His will, in His grace, in His love, and in His mercy, we watch and wait, knowing that the triumph and the victory will certainly be ours.

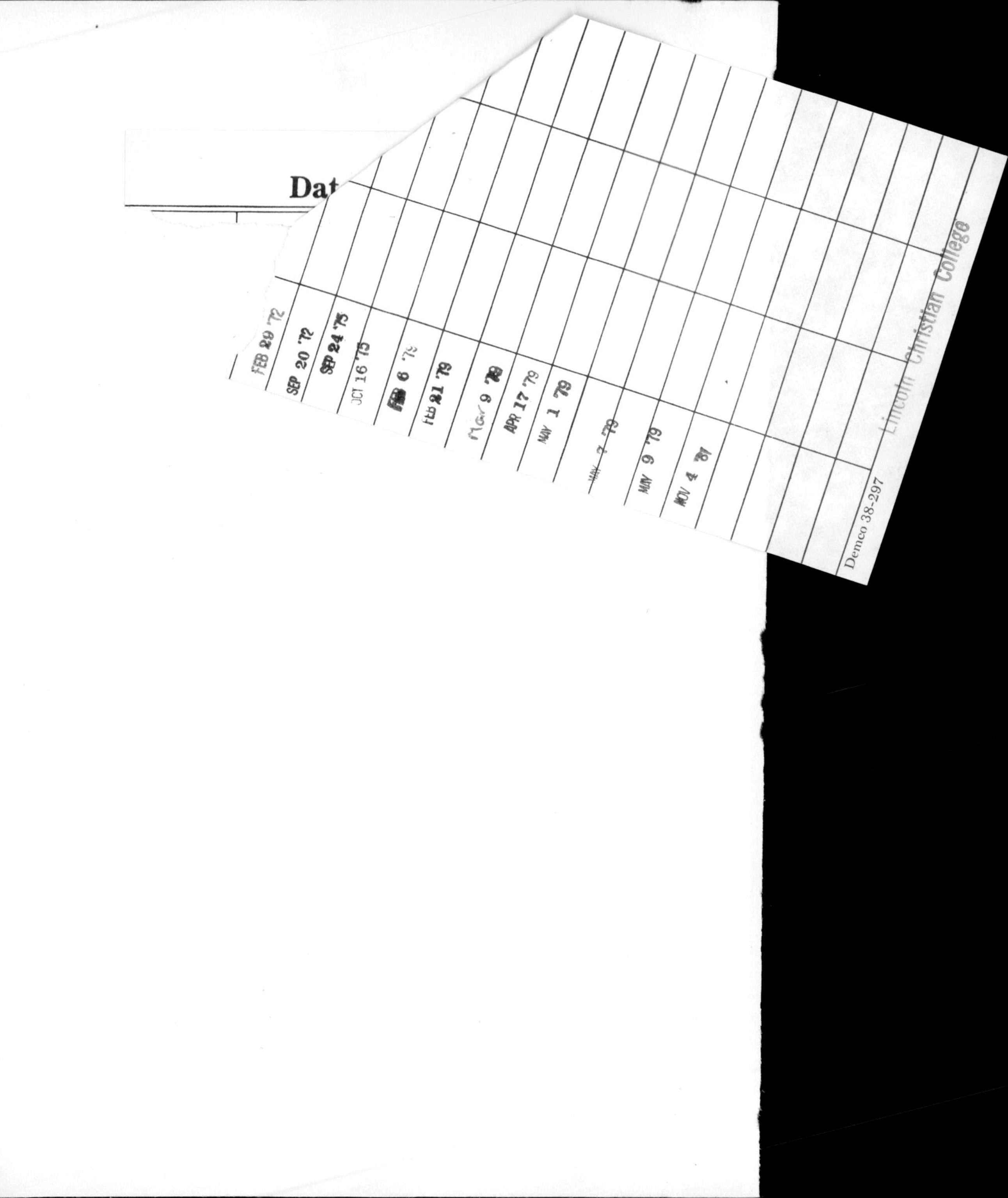
Dat
FEB 29 '72
SEP 20 '72
SEP 24 '75
OCT 16 '75
FEB 6 '79
FEB 21 '79
MAY 9 '79
APR 17 '79
MAY 1 '79
MAY 7 '79
MAY 9 '79
NOV 4 '81
Lincoln Christian College
Demco 38-297

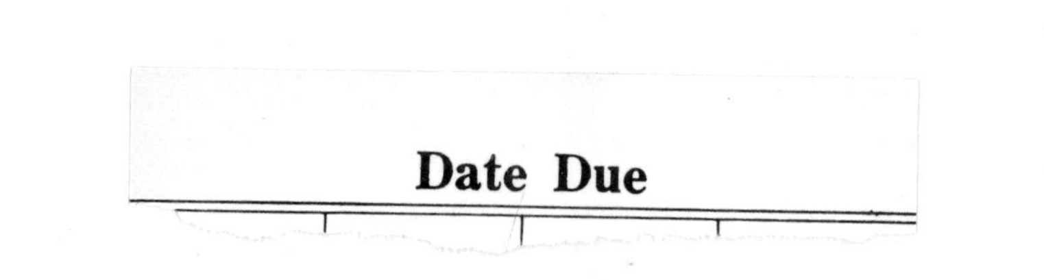
Date Due